Blessings
from MY CATS

How I Discovered
the Boundless
Joy of Caring
for Wild and
Domestic Strays

JANET S. DUMAS

Published by Who Chains You Publishing
P.O. Box 581
Amissville, VA 20106
www.WhoChainsYou.com

Cover and interior design by Tamira Thayne
tamirathayne.com

ISBN-13: 978-1-946044-57-0

Printed in the United States of America /

First Edition

DEDICATION

$\mathcal{T}$his book is in memoriam of the tens of thousands of innocent cats and dogs that were gassed to death by the City of San Antonio. The City later abandoned this cruel euthanasia method and—after a decade—achieved a no-kill status in 2015. I also dedicate this book to my fellow animal advocates who work tirelessly to improve the lives of cats and dogs in my community.

"My heart was touched by *Blessings From My Cats*; thank you, thank you for the lifeline you provide for so many cats and continuing to remind us of our spiritual connection to animals."—Sonya Fitzpatrick, Radio Show Host, SiriusXM, Animal Intuitive, TV Host of Animal Planet's "The Pet Psychic" and "Pet Psychic Encounters", Author, *What the Animals Tell Me* and *Cat Talk*

Praise for
BLESSINGS FROM MY CATS

"Blessings come in all shapes and sizes and often don't look like blessings at all. This very personal account of one woman's blessed relations with the cats in her life offers a good reminder to stay alert to the unexpected."—**Craig Brestrup**, PHD, Author, *Disposable Animals*

"In this collection of charming stories, Dumas captures an intimate relationship with cats, from those who share her home to those who rely on her care in the wild. Her insights will deliver a deeper understanding of the bond shared between people and cats."—**Cathy M. Rosenthal**, Author, *The Lucky Tale of Two Dogs*, Columnist, San Antonio Express News, "Animal Matters"

"A captivating, funny, and heart-warming story about the gratifying results of saving cats. It is also a wonderful 'how-to' book for feral and stray caretakers. The educational component is an added bonus! If only we had more 'Janets' out there." —**Sherry Derdak**, President, San Antonio Feral Cat Coalition

"It is always a joy to see all of the different ways that cats choose their people and then set about training them. It is a wonderful service, TNR, that Janet and her associates provide for the feral cat population of San Antonio. It gives me great satisfaction to be a small part of helping to improve the lives of these wonderful cats."—**Dr. Mike Mixon**, Founder of Texas Veterinary Hospitals

Contents

"MINDY"

Introduction

I have been a cat caretaker for more than thirty years; love for cats is part and parcel of my DNA. I grew up with two animal-loving parents, and in my memories we always housed at least one cat, one dog, a parakeet, and the occasional hamster. In fact, it was love at first sight for my parents when they met my first Persian cat, named Pasha. They thought of him as their grandcat, and began their telephone calls to me with, "How is Pasha?"

I thought they were kidding when they asked if Pasha could accompany them on their upcoming two-week RV trip. What kind of people ask to borrow another person's cat to take on a road trip? Two seniors who likened this request to asking a grandchild over to spend the night, that's who!

I couldn't bear the thought of being separated from my steadfast companion for so long, so I declined.

I regret that decision. Had I been able to foretell that their lives would be cut short in a matter of years, I would have packed up their grandcat with his favorite bed and toys and wished them all a fond farewell and bon voyage.

If you asked me if I would have predicted ten years ago that I would become the guardian of four stray cats and the caretaker of twenty-eight feral cats, I'd have responded with a resounding "No!" And yet today, here I am.

Just in case an explanation is needed, feral cats are those who have not been socialized to human touch. They live outdoors and are the offspring of stray or owned cats that are "intact" and allowed to roam free. Today I co-manage three feral cat colonies and carry the role of trapper and kitty transporter when they need medical care, too.

I naively wandered into feral cat advocacy when I saw three young kittens diving into a dumpster at one of my job sites. I thought my role would be to provide food, water, and to T-N-R (trap-neuter-return) the kittens, never anticipating the heartache that came along with the job—agonizing over life and death decisions, worrying about sick or missing cats, and experiencing profound grief upon having to euthanize them.

In short, I didn't consider that I would fall in love. After all, the cats were wild; how is it possible to fall in love with an animal that I can never touch, pet, cuddle, or kiss? Yet the cats quickly engaged me with their antics and unique personalities. And just as we fall in love with these alley cats, they in return form a loving bond with us as their caretakers.

My experiences with the cats have run the gamut from hysterical laughter at the gymnastics of tabby male LJ jumping onto "head cat" Toby—and then dismounting into a perfect somersault—to the profound sadness I felt when the dying male, Austin, made it clear he wanted to spend his last hours with me.

I myself hadn't heard the term feral cats, or barn cats in rural areas, until I went to community meetings and read literature from the San Antonio Feral Cat Coalition. I decided to attend the meetings as a way to do *something* after reading in the 2004 San Antonio Express-News about the 50,000 animals being euthanized each year by the City Animal Control Services Department [hereafter referred to as "the City"]. As unbelievable as it sounds, at that time the City was loaning traps to citizens to catch feral cats to deliver them to animal control for the express purpose of killing them. After reading the exposé, I felt outraged, helpless, and hopeless. For awhile, I couldn't even drive near the facility, and altered my driving routes to avoid being close to the torture chambers.

Learning about the plight of stray and feral cats in my city led me to feral cat colony management and, for the first time in my life, to the adoption of stray cats. I had been a Persian cat aficionado before this time; I couldn't resist their regal, if not snooty persona, the huge round eyes, and that long gorgeous fur coat. No mixed breed cats for me, no siree.

But then things changed, and I found myself understanding that my affection for cats didn't just extend to Persians—I loved them all. I have never gone to a shelter to adopt my stray cats—haven't needed to. Many of our citizens treat cats and dogs as disposable. Once they tire of the new puppy's chewing habits or discover that the new cat is pregnant, they simply toss the poor animals out into the street to fend for themselves. I have rescued five cats from my block alone. If I ever have a hankering for a new cat, I just have to walk outside my door.

Advocacy for stray and feral cats has become my avocation. Finding my passion in life has given me a fulfillment that I have never before experienced. On a typical Saturday two years ago, I was mentally reciting the chores on my "to do" list: sweep the deck, clean the carpet, wash clothes, write a book about cats. Whoa! Wait a minute. What was that fourth thing? I instantly knew that additional task had not come from me. To my knowledge, I hadn't even been thinking about writing a book. I believed it was more, a directive of divine origin.

And wouldn't you know, I heard that message in my head about ten more times that day. It filled my head again and again, every day and throughout the day for the next two weeks. I was listening to the messages, but in my attempt to absorb the meaning, I forgot to acknowledge that I'd heard the messages. My thoughts were occupied with contemplating how to carry out the edict. How would I go about writing a book? What would I include? When should I begin writing?

On the 14th day, after hearing the message all day long from morning until night, it dawned on me to acknowledge receiving the message. "Ok God, I get it. I hear you. I will write a book about my cats." I never heard the message again.

Some months and five chapters later, I was making the three-minute drive to church. A message filled my head: "You are to call the book *Blessings From My Cats*."

This time, I immediately answered. "What a perfect, beautiful title for my book. Thank you, thank you, thank you for naming the book." I'd been stumped as to what to call the project; I had a few ideas but nothing that really grabbed me. But this was the exactly right title! I never heard the message again.

And so here we are, finally, and you have a copy of *Blessings from My Cats* in hand. I hope you enjoy reading it as much as I enjoyed choosing and telling their stories.

I'm the first to admit that stray and feral cat advocacy is not for the faint of heart. The gut-wrenching loss of my feral cats and the grief I carry for cats that have gone missing weigh heavily on my heart. I say with the utmost conviction that the emotional highs far surpass the lows, and those rewards fuel my commitment to the cats.

Their unwavering will to survive is extraordinary. It is gratifying to know that my efforts improve and extend their lives. I hope that my experiences will inspire appreciation for the intrinsic value of these alley cats and inspire others to care for them and to love them. As I daily contemplate the many blessings in my life, I would be remiss to not reflect upon the blessings from my cats.

PART ONE
My Feral Cats

"MISSY"

"DADDY"

Chapter 1
CRUEL KILLING

My interest in feral cats began after reading the *San Antonio Express-News* "Death By The Pound" series[1] about the cruel, tortuous "wholesale killing" of dogs and cats by the City Animal Control Department. San Antonio was killing 50,000 animals per year at that time, more per capita than any other major city, with only a 10% live release rate. Not

1 Lisa Sandberg, "Death by the Pound," *San Antonio Express-News* November 14-15, 2004

only was the "catch and kill" mentality of the city inhumane and outrageous, the means of the killing was equally horrific.

Animals went to the gas chamber, by that time a rare, archaic means of animal euthanasia. City control workers told the newspaper reporters of quickly leaving the gas chambers to avoid hearing the wailing of the terrified dogs and cats locked inside, knowing death was coming for them. The protocol of checking the animal's vital signs after the gassing and before transferring the body to a truck to be taken to a dump was routinely *not* followed. Many animals were essentially buried alive.

It's hard to describe the myriad of emotions I felt after reading this series. I read the articles through buckets of tears, often putting the paper aside because I simply couldn't take one more word of horror. I felt outrage and disbelief toward our City leaders for allowing this. I felt an achingly profound sadness and sympathy for the innocent victims—the animals.

For the first time in my life, I felt ashamed to be a native San Antonioan. I wondered what tourists would think of their beloved Alamo City and world-famous river walk if they knew this dirty little secret. I recalled a quote by Mahatma Gandhi: "The greatness of a nation and its moral progress can be judged by the way its animals are treated."

The exposé generated a collective response from numerous animal advocacy groups who approached the City about partnering to create a comprehensive plan to increase the City's live release numbers. As a result of the exposure and subsequent pressure, the City launched an initiative to become a no-kill facility by 2012. In fiscal year 2010, 18,000 animals were euthanized by lethal injection. While this is a notable improvement from 2004, seventy-five percent of the animals taken in that year were euthanized.

The City has made progress by implementing an adoption and foster program, as well as free and low-cost spay and neuter incentives. Local and national partnerships now fund about 50,000 annual low-cost or free spay/neuter surgeries. Local animal advocates estimate we need to almost double that number to achieve no-kill status.

The City made steady progress by implementing an adoption and foster program, as well as free and low-cost spay and neuter, resulting in about 50,000 annual surgeries. They then added mobile spay/neuter services that visit the areas of the city with the largest number of stray dogs. The sheer number of stray dogs on our streets, estimated at 200,000, and the limited space at the city shelter represented a particular challenge. To address this, a campaign to encourage spay/neuter and adoption was launched, with messages featured via radio, TV, social media, spay and neuter clinics, pet fairs, and workshops.

The City held a number of town hall meetings after the newspaper series. Various dog and cat rescue/

advocacy groups attended those meetings and city council hearings. They formed a coalition that is still active and making a difference in the lives of homeless animals in San Antonio. They regularly host adoption fairs and mobilize volunteers to foster animals. Moreover, the various dog breed rescue groups routinely remove dogs from the City facility to place for adoption. It was at one of the community meetings that I learned about the challenges of the vast number of stray and feral cats in San Antonio.

As I said previously, at that time the City Animal Control Department allowed folks to capture feral cats and deliver them to the City to be killed. The City even loaned out the traps to catch the poor, innocent creatures. I would later hear a lecture by a national expert who consults with municipalities to develop no-kill strategies. Among his proven methods for helping cities achieve this goal was a simple and logical philosophy for dealing with feral cats.

City shelters have no business accepting an animal that is not adoptable. Which, of course, is the defining feature of a feral cat: they are unadoptable. A feral cat is a cat born outside that is not socialized to human touch, and, with the exception of young kittens, will never become socialized.

He advised that feral cats should not be captured and killed. They should be afforded "protective wildlife" status. This was such a simple philosophy that I wondered why more municipalities had not adopted this commonsense approach. He further explained that the primary strategy for cities striving to kill fewer animals is simply to decrease the number of animals that come in.

In fiscal year 2011, San Antonio had a live release rate of 32% and this increased to 61% in 2012. While the City didn't reach its ambitious no-kill goal by 2012, that accomplishment was realized in December 2015. The standard for no-kill designation requires a live release rate of at least 90%. Reaching no-kill status was a complex process that continues to involve the entire community. Citizens need to become more responsible pet owners by embracing the philosophy of spay/neuter.

Today, the City maintains its no-kill status through numerous partnerships with local and national shelters, local and national rescue/animal advocacy groups, and with philanthropic and corporate charitable foundations.

"Toby"

Chapter 2
Meet the Ferals

When I started caring for the feral cats at one of my job sites, I never imagined that I would become so attached to them. How could I develop a loving relationship with a cat that I can't hold in my arms? But I learned feral cats all possess and display their own distinct personalities and antics, just as socialized "owned" cats do. And, just as we grow to love them, they learn to trust and bond with us too.

Toby is the "head cat" at the feral cat colony. She is a beautiful grey and white cat with short hair and green eyes. More than one person has commented on what a beautiful face she has. One of my first priorities in managing the colony was to put into practice my newly-honed trapping skills, recently acquired through the free Trap-Neuter-Return (TNR) course sponsored by the San Antonio Feral Cat Coalition.

My goal was to start with the two adult female cats, Toby and Maggie. I decided I would trap Toby first. We'd already established a strong bond by the time I was set to trap her, and catching her proved easier than I'd hoped. My first success!

Then things went awry. After bringing her home, I transferred her to a cage in my garage for a two-day stay until I could get her to the spay/neuter clinic on Monday. Much to my chagrin, I had not properly secured the new crate, and she escaped into my garage. As a novice trapper, I had not yet learned about the practice of "re-trapping" an escaped animal. To make a long story short, Toby escaped from my garage.

When I tell people this story, most are initially not troubled about her leaving the garage. They erroneously believe that a lost feral cat will be fine, that someone else will feed her. I knew it wouldn't be so easy for Toby outside the protective confines of the colony where she had come to depend on a steady supply of food and water. She was not homeless. She had a home.

And, she had a cat family. I worried about how scared and hungry she would be, wandering around in unfamiliar territory. I was devastated. I loved that little girl. I was wracked with guilt. How could I have so badly bungled my first feral cat trapping?

I thought about Toby every time I visited the colony for my feeding and watering chores. I was still blaming myself when one day, about two weeks after Toby had gone missing, there was an amazing turn of events. While I was at the colony feeding the cats, my gaze wandered to a nearby underground drainage ditch. For a fleeting second, I thought I saw Toby's head emerge from the ground level crevice. Were my eyes playing tricks on me? I moved closer to get a better look at the kitty. I was 100% certain. Toby had come home.

We've all heard stories about lost cats and dogs who inexplicably return to their homes after going missing. I never thought I would experience this, first hand, with one of my animals. I cried with happiness and called my friend Chris to share the amazing news. He was nearly speechless. At the time, Chris taught trap-neuter-return classes for the San Antonio Feral Cat Coalition, and he began to include this story in the part of the curriculum that covers how not to lose your cat. The anecdote never failed to inspire and delight his students. I am the only person I know who has had a lost pet find her way back home.

I am still amazed today about her return. I live in

the heart of San Antonio, among congested streets and freeways. How did Toby navigate the three-mile journey from my home to the colony? She had several route options, but each one would have been equally perilous, requiring her to cross an underpass of a very busy freeway. Even driving my SUV around town, with thousands of pounds of protective steel surrounding me, I am keenly aware that crossing Loop 410 can be treacherous. For Toby to have survived this dangerous crossing is nothing short of a miracle.

Since I lost Toby that day, I'm happy to report that T-N-R protocol no longer requires the trapper to transfer the captured cat from a trap to a different crate. The feline can receive pre-operative care and post-surgery recovery in the same, humane trap. No more lost cats!

Life continued on at the feral cat colony, but I would not be successful at trapping Toby again for some time. She'd become trap savvy. All TNR practitioners know and understand that you pretty much have one shot at trapping a feral, and I'd blown my chance.

I decided to consult with world-renowned animal communicator Sonya Fitzpatrick, hoping she could assist me by explaining to Toby that I was trying to help her. I was familiar with Sonya from my 20 years living in Houston, where she currently resides. I knew of a number of Houstonians who had consulted her and been very pleased with the outcome. I'd also been a loyal fan of her Animal Planet series, "The Pet

Psychic", so I went into the with a positive attitude and my fingers crossed.

I followed the instructions on her website for scheduling a telephone appointment and sent a photo of Toby with an explanation of my goals for the consultation. I was not prepared at all for what would ensue. It's hard to put into words my feelings about how incredible and rewarding the experience was for me. To be able to hear what your pets are thinking and to communicate with them? Thrilling! I didn't at all anticipate the myriad of emotions that would spill out.

Before Sonya could explain to Toby the purpose of the conversation, Toby opened up the dialogue by saying how much she and the other cats appreciated me taking care of them. The feline had a lot to say. She told Sonya I had made their lives so much easier. She was especially thankful that I came to feed them regularly, *"no matter what kind of weather."* That comment really moved me in that she acknowledged my commitment to them.

Toby lives at one of the retirement communities I represent in my sales role for a national senior living company. She mentioned that she didn't think I was a nurse like some of the other staff because I didn't wear a uniform. She guessed that I must be an office worker. She said most of the residents and staff were nice to her and the other cats. She assured Sonya that she knew it was important to stay away from cars. I thought that was a very sweet and astute comment for Toby to make—to assure me that she conducts herself safely among the many cars that come and go at that location.

She told Sonya that she had stayed at my home for a short time, but that she returned to the colony because the other cats depended on her. Sonya said Toby described her position in the colony as sort of the "head cat" that looks after all the other cats. Sonya then explained to Toby that I wanted to help her by preventing her from having more kittens, and that this would require her to be away from the colony for a couple of days. Sonya assured Toby I would return her to her home afterward.

It would be another year before I was able to re-trap and spay Ms. Toby. Thanks to the Ally Cat Allies website, I learned about various ways to successfully trap cats that have become trap savvy like Toby. The website contains numerous examples for disguising the traps. The method that helped me to finally catch Toby again was to completely cover the trap with freshly cut shrubbery.

Before I caught her again, though, Toby had another litter of three kittens. I trapped and fostered her babies and was able to get them all into good homes. I found a wonderful place for the female kitten right away. She had beautiful grey and white markings and green eyes. She was practically a clone of Toby, and she had her mom's sweet and outgoing personality as well.

As part of my marketing campaign to find homes for the remaining two kittens, I hand-delivered advertising photos and flyers to my customers. I also did an email blast to my social and business contacts. I named the male orange and white kittens Tommy and Travis, and they were both sweet, healthy boys.

I decided to take photos to one of my physician customers, Dr. Melba Beine. I knew she was a cat lover, so I felt pretty safe in asking for her help with my marketing campaign. I was unable to personally meet with her, so I left my request with her receptionist. About a week later, I returned to her office to follow up; I was bowled over and so grateful to see the photos of the kittens and the promotional flyer prominently displayed on the door leading to the patient suites!

Then, about a week later, I ran into her clinic marketer at a networking event. I mentioned how much I appreciated that Dr. Beine was willing to help publicize my kitten adoption campaign.

I unknowingly hit a nerve. The marketing representative explained that she had recently hung a poster on that very door to promote an upcoming event for their patients. She was dismayed to see that the poster had been removed and replaced with photographs of some cats. She said "some cats" with noticeable irritation, intimating disgust that photos of some unknown, wretched, homeless cats could end up on her clinic door.

"So you are responsible for this," she said to me in an annoyed, accusatory tone.

After a few tense moments of uncomfortable silence, we both had a good laugh. I apologized that my request for help had interfered with her marketing plans. I was immensely grateful for Dr. Beine's support, and even though I got into trouble with the marketer, I was secretly cheering for the doctor's sales savvy. I said to myself, "Way to go, Dr. Beine!"

Tommy and Travis were eventually adopted by my then-boyfriend, John. He lives in the country and cares for a large feral cat colony that resides on his one-acre property. It was very satisfying to watch the two boys assimilate into the group. We gradually introduced the kittens to the principal cats, who enjoyed the boisterous youngsters and had great fun teaching them the ropes.

Fritz and Cat taught the boys how to climb to the roof. Tommy, the more outgoing and daring of the siblings, learned roof climbing quicker than his more timid brother. The lessons included a primer on how to follow the sun around the wraparound deck throughout the day to ensure the best times for capturing warmth.

That being settled, it was now time to do more trapping at the colony. There remained one intact female I called Maggie, a short-haired tortoiseshell with golden eyes. Previous attempts at trapping

Maggie had been unsuccessful. I asked my friend Chris, our local expert, to assist me in trapping the ever-elusive cat. Maggie had become the bane of my existence! I was convinced she was the Houdini of the cat world. I'd tried every cat trap disguise trick known to man, and she remained one step ahead of me.

One time, Maggie went into the trap, triggered the trap door, and then managed to escape before the trap door slammed shut behind her. I'd never seen or heard of anything like that. Chris reacted to this story with a nonchalant, "Oh yeah, I had one like that, too, and that's why we'll be using the 'trap of last resort'."

I still laugh when I hear this label. Oh yeah, this was definitely a scenario for the "trap of last resort"! Bring it on . . .

The trap of last resort, officially called the drop trap, is much larger than a conventional trap. It allows the cat to come in, feed, and freely leave. Cats see other cats come and go and are not afraid to enter the trap. In trapping ferals with a conventional trap, you run the risk of trapping the wrong cat. With this trap, the trap door is manually triggered from a distance once the target cat enters the trap. Brilliant!

We did not catch Maggie that day. I later discovered the cats had been fed the previous day and were not hungry enough to come into the trap. Withholding food from the cats the day prior to trapping is my least favorite part of trapping, but this standard practice increases the chances for success.

No one ever said taking care of a feral cat colony is easy. While the experience brings immeasurable joy and rewards most days, sometimes there is sadness. The father of Toby's kittens approached me one day while I was trapping. Janice and I had noticed his declining weight in the previous weeks. We knew he was sick, and we were very worried about him.

I had been unsuccessful in trapping him over the years. He was the "Big Man on Campus," responsible for fathering a number of litters. As a beautiful, short-haired orange tabby, he had sired some beautiful babies. He was as feral as the day is long, always maintaining a safe distance of at least fifty feet from his human caretakers.

Now he was painfully thin and obviously sick. His feral fear of me was gone. He walked right up to me, slowly and with an unsteady gait. His meow was very weak as he asked for food. I leaned down and talked to him, and he still showed no fear. I picked him up and placed him in the trap where he could have a little food. I instinctively felt that he wanted to come with me, so I brought him home, painfully aware then that our head male cat was dying.

I transferred him to a cage and offered him high-nutrition cat food. He ate perhaps one tablespoon and stood for a short time. Over the next few hours, I spoke tenderly to him, petted him, kissed him, and told him how handsome he was. I told him all about his kitten Haley, how she came to live with me, how much I loved her, and how well she was doing.

I also briefed him on his other offspring—Tommy, Travis and their beautiful sister who had been adopted by a family from Boerne. I told him I was happy for the privilege of caring for him these past few years. He peacefully passed away several hours later.

I was profoundly saddened at his death. I didn't realize I had become so emotionally attached to him, especially since he was one of the more skittish colony residents. I was stunned and at the same time honored that this kitty wanted my companionship in the few remaining hours of his life.

I never knew he felt he had a relationship with me. I likewise did not realize that I had grown to love him. I posthumously named him Austin, and decided to also bestow a name to his kitten that had died Christmas Day—I named his son Austin Jr.

I believe that life is good for my precious alley cats. Toby remains the maternal head cat and has become somewhat of a mascot at the retirement community. She regularly shows her gratitude and love for me in various ways. She comes perilously close, within 6-10 feet, rolling around on her back in a flirtatious invitation to pet her. My colony co-manager Janice also observes this behavior. However, just as we get within touching distance, she moves away, suddenly remembering that she is feral and afraid of us.

Toby also shows her affection by giving us plenty of "eye squeezes", or opening and closing her eyes in rapid succession when we talk to her. She knows my car and runs over to the feeding station as soon as she sees me drive up. On sunny days, she can usually be seen basking, alone or with one of her companions. The elusive Maggie, the mother of my cat Haley, is very shy. Maggie has surprised me recently by slowly shortening the distance of her comfort zone.

The current cast of characters is quite an amicable group. In addition to Toby and Maggie, we have Chloe, a solid black Manx, and a new short-haired, caramel-colored cat. I believe his left ear has been tipped, which would indicate he'd been neutered.

I was able to watch him briefly through my binoculars on a subsequent trapping expedition. When I say briefly, I mean briefly. He runs for the hills if either of us gets within 100 feet of him! Janice commented that he runs so fast, she sees the blur of his hind legs galloping away, much like one sees the hind legs of a scampering rabbit.

Due to his skittish behavior, we haven't yet been able to fully confirm the ear tip. The spay/neuter process for ferals includes the notching of the cat's left ear. This process is a universal indication to feral colony caretakers and clinics that a cat has been neutered. I initially and naively didn't understand the practicality of this protocol, until I had more than one tabby in the same colony. The ear marking helped me to identify which of the nearly identical green-eyed females had already been spayed.

Unfortunately, two of our females have disappeared in recent months. Mindy was a two-year-old tabby with huge green eyes who we believe was Maggie's offspring. These two kitties lived at the back of the property and used a storage shed for shelter. The property manager had the openings in the shed repaired, and this eliminated the cats' access to the structure. I instinctively knew this would severely disrupt their routine.

Within a few days the cats vanished, which was very upsetting to me as I was attached to Mindy. The other cat, Abby, and her eight-week-old kittens had arrived only recently. Abby was a tortie like Maggie, and no doubt an unintended by-product of my unsuccessful attempts at trapping Maggie. I worry about the missing felines. Janice believes the two siblings and the kittens moved as a family to another colony or that someone is feeding them in the residential neighborhood behind the property. I pray that all of them are okay and they haven't met an ill fate. It is excruciating to lose these cats after developing such a close bond with them.

I recently noticed a new male cat while conducting my feeding chores. He is an orange and white tabby with an injured eye. His eye is draining, and has the light-colored glassy look of a blind eye. My heart sank when I saw this. Since he is still an intact "tom," we are guessing his eye was injured in a cat fight, or he is suffering from a severe eye infection.

Intellectually, I knew that sooner or later an injured cat would join the group. Now that it has happened, the emotional reality of being confronted with this kind of dilemma creates a whole new ballgame. I have to force myself to focus on the positive.

I am improving his quality of life by providing him with ample food and water. I intend to help him further by getting him neutered. But how to handle a sick feral? This is new territory for me.

Should I trap him and take him to the veterinarian that treats my household cats? Would he even be able to treat a feral cat? I didn't know.

"Maggie"

Chapter 3
Maggie and LJ

I t was weeks after our first encounter when I again saw the new orange male with the glassy eye. The eye had not improved. It was time to take him to a veterinarian. I'd never taken a feral cat in for medical treatment, so this would be a challenge, to be sure. He needed to be neutered anyway, so this would provide an opportunity for evaluation and treatment while he was under sedation for the neuter procedure.

I called the office of Dr. Mike Mixon and spoke with the senior tech about my desire to have him assess the kitty. I asked her if she thought this sounded like a reasonable goal. She agreed that yes, at the very least Doc Mixon could diagnose the eye condition and discuss appropriate treatment options in light of his feral status. I began praying to God and St. Francis of Assisi, the patron saint of animals, for guidance to assist me with trapping the cat.

I decided this would also be another opportunity to try yet again to catch the enigmatic Maggie. The tortoiseshell feline had become my biggest trapping challenge since beginning my feral cat advocacy. I added Maggie to my prayerful appeal to St. Francis. I had worried about Maggie for several years, aware that she must have borne several litters of kittens. Because of the high mortality of feral kittens, I assumed the majority of her kittens had not survived. This has weighed heavily on me. I have mourned the certain deaths of her babies and the cruel cycle that nature perpetuates on intact females. I recently figured out that some of the cats that joined the colony during this time were Maggie's surviving adult kittens.

I asked my friend Chris to assist me in this dual trapping challenge. He agreed, and we made plans to trap the cats early Monday morning. He was still in possession of the drop trap, aka the trap of last resort, and our strategy was to use the drop trap for the trap savvy Maggie and a conventional trap for the male.

The gang was all there when we arrived. I'd withheld food the previous day so the cats would be hungry, which I hated doing, but the ends justified the means. Maggie was one of the first cats to approach the traps. She smelled the tuna and briefly investigated the drop trap. Then she promptly ran in the opposite direction!

I sighed and told Chris, "Now you see what I've been dealing with." He laughed and asked me to be patient.

I set out the conventional trap, and the waiting game began. Maggie was now hundreds of yards away, sunning herself and taking her morning bath. She showed no signs of returning to the trap zone. I was discouraged and began praying.

To pass the time and ease my anxiety, I returned to my car and checked my email on my blackberry. Chris dutifully remained near both traps. About 30 minutes passed when I heard the large door of the drop trap snap closed. What?!

I looked up and almost couldn't believe my eyes: Maggie was in the drop trap! I bolted from my car and met Chris at the trap, just as he was about to throw a sheet over it to help ease her stress.

I was almost shaking, my voice stuttering as I asked for confirmation. "Is that . . . is that Maggie in the trap?" With my history of failed Maggie trappings, I was afraid to believe it was really her.

Chris grinned widely and said, "Yes, we got your cat."

I was so happy that tears filled my eyes as I thanked him. I know I surprised him by grabbing him and hugging him. My voice broke as I told him how worried I had been about her all these years, at risk of getting pregnant and bearing kittens.

He smiled and said, "But listen, you've taken good care of her all this time. Remember that." His words were very reassuring, just what I needed to hear.

I wasn't prepared for the myriad of emotions that spilled out of me after trapping Maggie. I'd been on an emotional roller coaster with this feline since day one; now all those pent up emotions struck me at once. I was feeling some weird mixture of excitement, happiness, disbelief, and relief. On top of that was the adrenaline rush that comes with a successful trapping—the knowledge that you'd finally done it. I just couldn't believe it!

Feral cat advocates know that the #1 rule of trapping is that you pretty much have only one shot at it. This creates a whirlwind of anxiety and other stress-filled emotions during the preparation and trapping attempt. The cats who manage to escape the conventional traps—as Maggie did—have a long memory of that experience. These cats in essence become nearly impossible to catch after that.

With Maggie now safely secured in a trap, we next turned our attention to the second cat on our radar.

Within minutes of trapping Maggie, the orange tabby with the injured eye entered the other trap— an easy catch! As far as trapping excursions go, this session had produced remarkably fast results. We caught our two target cats within a little over an hour, and I was feeling euphoric. My celebratory mood gave way to anxiety as I pondered how the appointment for the orange tabby would go with Dr. Mixon. What was the nature of the cat's eye injury? Would Dr. Mike be able to successfully resolve the problem?

I couldn't wait to phone my sister with the successful results of my trapping excursion. I shared with her how I had called on God and St. Francis to help me trap the two cats. After hearing all the details and sharing her happiness with me, she asked, "Do you know what day today is?"

I said I knew it was Monday, October 4th.

She answered, "Today is the Feast day of St. Francis of Assisi."

Ah! Well, that explained the miracle of trapping Maggie. I described how upon inspecting the traps, Maggie had run in the opposite direction—typical Maggie behavior. All the other times Maggie had run away from the traps, she'd never returned. I believe that St. Francis directed her into the trap; the successful capture of those two significant prospects in one day was nothing short of providential.

Still reeling from the emotions I felt after capturing our elusive girl, I was stressing over one more issue that wouldn't be resolved until the following day: could she be pregnant or nursing kittens now? I prayed as I took Maggie to the spay-neuter clinic the next morning, and I anxiously awaited her post-surgery report. Thanks be to God, she was neither.

I knew it would have been disastrous to take a nursing mom away from her young kittens for two days; and, if she'd been pregnant, I didn't want to go through the emotions of having her pregnancy terminated.

I also dropped the orange male off at Dr. Mixon's clinic for the neuter procedure and eye examination. Dr. Mike called me a few hours later with his assessment. The cat's eyeball had been punctured in a fight, and the dead eye tissue was necrosing. This explained the drainage we had seen; he'd already lost the vision in that eye.

The only treatment option was an enucleation—removal of the eye. Without that procedure, infection would claim his life. I had felt in my gut that his injury was beyond repair, so I promptly gave Dr. Mixon the needed permission to proceed. Doc Mixon explained the procedure, the post surgery protocol, and expected recovery time. He told me the cat's eye socket would be swollen for a couple of days, but I wouldn't see the sutures as he'd hidden them under the eyelid.

I couldn't allow him to get cold, because a sedated cat can't regulate his body temperature. Doctor Mike estimated that the sedation would wear off within three days. He told me he'd gone heavy on the medications to ease the cat's recovery and my ability to care for him, given his feral status. I should plan to foster him from three to five days.

Janice met me at my home that afternoon. I had two feral cats in my possession that needed short-term fostering. We agreed she would foster Maggie, and I would foster the orange male. It is recommended that spayed females be fostered for at least forty-eight hours before being returned to the feral cat colony. We loaded Maggie into her car, and Janice helped me transfer our male into his temporary quarters in my garage.

We settled in for the long haul.

All seemed to go well for the first day and a half. But then, two days post surgery, I became alarmed when I observed spots of blood on the floor of the crate and dried blood on the kitty's face. I could also distinctly see an incision line around the eye socket. I didn't think I was supposed to see that.

I called Doc Mixon and described what I was seeing. He said it was normal for the eye socket to drain for several days post surgery. I asked him if he would consider making a house call since I lived so close to the clinic. He came by that evening on his way home from work.

He looked at the kitty and declared that the wound looked fantastic! He admitted that he'd been a bit concerned about what he would find; from my report, it sounded like the sutures had pulled apart. I felt bad that I'd alarmed him with my amateur medical observation skills. He was kind and patient as he educated me, telling me it was normal to see the incision but not the hidden sutures—I'd been mistaken in thinking that's what I was seeing.

Admittedly, it will forever remain a medical mystery to me how the incision was visible while the sutures were hidden, but I decided this fits into the realm of life mysteries I don't need to understand but rather just accept.

This boy turned out to be was very easy to care for. He didn't hiss or growl at me, even in the beginning. I believe this demonstrated that he felt he had a relationship with me, that he knew I was trying to help him and he trusted me. After I settled him into his crate, I told him with a quivering voice that his eye was too sick to be saved. I explained that the nice doctor had saved his life by removing his eye, and I told him that in a few days he would not feel any more pain. I reassured him also that I would reunite him with his cat family.

It was time to name this kitty. I decided on LJ, after the chief investigator on the television program

"NCIS." The team leader's name is Leroy Jethro Gibbs, but everyone except his father calls him Gibbs. His father's nickname for him is LJ.

Gibbs is a scrappy ex-marine and war veteran who proudly wears his emotional and physical battle scars. Dr. Mike assessed that LJ was not a young cat, and we both surmised he'd been on the streets his entire life. LJ the cat was very bit as much a survivor as his television namesake.

LJ's eye socket drained only that one day, and the rest of his recovery was thankfully unremarkable. I released him after five full days when I was certain his appetite was back to normal and he was in full control of all his faculties. Janice and I see him regularly at the colony, and he looks good. As fastidious as cats are about grooming, he quickly cleaned off all the dried blood from his face, and his surgical wound continued to heal nicely.

If he hadn't been feral, post surgery instructions would have included wiping his face daily with a warm wash cloth. He will go through a period of adjustment to life with one eye, but overall his life will improve. Now that he is neutered, the male tendency toward aggression and fighting will be greatly reduced, and he will no longer be competing with other males for available females.

Neutered males are also less aggressive about protecting their turf. We will never know if he lost his eye fighting over a female or fighting for entry into the colony.

Capturing both Maggie and LJ made for the most productive and satisfying week of my feral cat advocacy. It was, hands down, also the most stressful week of my feral cat adventures. I had a difficult time de-stressing from the emotional events of the week. I dealt with the stress several evenings that week by celebrating at happy hour with margaritas. I also went to my favorite restaurant for take-out Mexican food; thanks to God for creating Mexican food and margaritas!

"DADDY"

Chapter 4
FATHER AND DAUGHTER REUNION

During the Christmas holidays, my coworker Christina emailed me to tell me some new cats had taken up residence in a community behind the medical center in our area. This is the same community that houses the second feral cat colony that I manage. Oh, no! Could I take on even more?

The original family of cats resides at the front of the community. Christina wanted to know what we could do to help this new batch of cats. Over the course of a few conversations, I advised her that we would need to put in place both a short term and long term care strategy. We would need folks willing to regularly feed and water the cats, and she advised me she'd already assumed this responsibility. I told her it would be important to put a TNR plan in place, but I would volunteer to handle the trapping and neutering as I do for my other two colonies, as long as I was sure someone else was handling the daily feeding and care.

I asked Christina to describe for me the makeup of the colony. It appeared we had one adult male, two adult females, and two sets of kittens of varying ages. All in all, we figured we had about six new cats. I told her I would meet her at the community over the next day or two. I find it helps me to see the cats to establish a priority for trapping purposes.

I would assess for signs of a pregnant female and try to determine the ages of the kittens for spay/neuter planning. Upon seeing our new charges, I was relieved to see that neither of the adult females appeared to be currently pregnant. One of the kittens appeared to be a male or female about four months old, and there was a male sibling the same age, as well as a younger male that was obviously the only remaining kitten from the second adult female.

I was immediately struck by what a handsome and diverse group of felines they were, from a coloring perspective. Our cats at the front of the property don't have much color diversity—three of them are solid back and one is solid grey. This new group consisted of a grey and white tabby papa, a grey and white female tabby kitten, a solid grey mom, a solid grey male kitten with white paws, a calico female, and a very handsome orange and white tabby male kitten.

The male kitten with the white paws was quickly and aptly christened "Socks." He was adopted by one of our associates after he successfully completed a week long "Kitten Socialization 101" stay with Christina and her husband.

I decided my trapping priority would be the two adult females first. However, six weeks and three trapping sessions later, and I had yet to catch those wily moms. My friend Chris accompanied me on one of these trapping outings. He commented how much easier it is to trap males than females because, as he put it, "the females are just a lot smarter than the males, and hence more leery of the traps."

That was a light bulb moment for me. I'd never stopped to consider that out of all the kitties that have been the most challenging to trap, 100% of them have been of the female persuasion. I believe he has an accurate perception of feline male and female intelligence.

Trapping the grey and white female kitten proved to be unremarkable. The events following her capture would, on the other hand, prove to be entirely remarkable. Christina named her Sally. I fostered Sally for two days following her surgery as per the foster protocol for females. She was a very easy patient— never hissing, never growling, and never "tossing" her cage.

Tossing the cage is when the cat completely turns over and empties all the food, litter, and water containers, a stress response to being captured. Instead, I was struck by how sad she looked. She seemed lethargic and depressed by her ordeal.

Going into the second day, Sally stopped eating. I knew her lack of appetite was not a complication from the surgery, as there were no signs of bleeding on the bottom of the cage. My gut instinct told me she had stopped eating due to the stress of being away from her cat family.

The fear of being caged in strange surroundings was another factor, and I could only imagine how terrifying that must be to a being used to complete freedom. Even so, I had fostered numerous ferals over the past five years, and I'd never before had one quit eating. It was upsetting. I don't know what I would have done if she'd needed to stay with me for an even longer period of time.

Fortunately, by the end of the second day, it was time to release her. I transported her in the cage and my coworker Deb met me at the colony to help me move the cage from my SUV to the ground. We placed the crate on the ground and I opened the cage door.

Most cats bolt out of the cage door within seconds . . . not our Sally. She didn't move a muscle and looked frozen with fright.

I then removed the sheet that had been covering about two thirds of the cage, thinking maybe she needed to get a 360-degree view to realize she was home. Nope. She remained glued to the bottom of the crate.

This was all rather vexing.

I told Deb maybe we needed to step further away from the cage. We did that. Sally still wouldn't budge. I must have sounded like a broken record telling Deb over and over again how confounded I was, never having seen a cat take so long to vacate a cage.

About this time, her cat daddy came around the corner. He did a slow, luxurious cat stretch as he surveyed his kingdom. He must have just gotten up from a nap. Christina had named our male patriarch "Daddy".

Daddy soon spotted Sally in the crate. Without any hesitation or fear of us, he started moving closer. It seemed like he wanted to get a better look. I was stunned when he very deliberately walked directly over to the cage, placing himself very close to us. I remember thinking that he must have momentarily forgotten that he was feral and afraid of humans. I could just imagine him thinking, *"Hey, that's one of my kiddos. I wondered where she had gone. I better go over and check this out."*

He stood at the entrance to the cage and peered in at his kitten. He was inches away from her face. Her head was turned away from him and she was completely oblivious to his presence. Deb commented on the resemblance between father and daughter. Both are gorgeous grey and white tabbies with large green eyes. I remember commenting to Deb about how stressed and afraid Sally must be feeling. She wasn't moving a muscle, completely unaware that Daddy was almost touching her.

Daddy also noticed he was unable to get his daughter's attention. He decided this called for a bolder, more brazen approach. He stuck his head inside the cage. This still elicited no response from little Sally. Deb and I were on pins and needles watching the drama unfold and wondering what would happen next.

Daddy then took his intervention a step further. Just as he was beginning to climb into the crate, daughter Sally finally sensed his presence. She turned her head and saw him, and that recognition was her green light. She realized she was home! She bolted from the crate, and he ran along right after her.

Deb and I had to take a few minutes to process what had just happened. I felt excited and privileged to have witnessed this level of animal communication. I had never observed a welcome home greeting among feral cats. I interpreted his actions to mean several things. I believe we observed some important behavioral aspects of colony life. The cats clearly have unique relationships with each other. They care for one another and look after each other as members of a family.

Daddy was keenly aware that daughter Sally was missing from the group. He recognized her as his kitten and as a cherished member of the Pride. He wanted to greet her and welcome her back. I relayed this story to Christina, and she was very moved. Christina had mentioned to me several times before this incident that Daddy frequently socializes with all his kittens. I remember upon first hearing about Daddy's parenting activities that I felt this behavior seemed unusual for an adult male cat. I would never have guessed that Daddy's affection for his kittens would have extended to the level of involvement that he displayed with Sally.

This was a very poignant ending to my fostering experience with little Sally. Sally and Daddy are both thriving along with the other members of their little family. Daddy continues to demonstrate his outgoing personality, and he has become socialized to the extent that when Christina arrives to feed the cats, he meows, meets her at her car and accompanies her to their bowls.

Chapter 5
FOUND AND LOST

D uring those first few weeks of learning about our newest feral cat colony, Christina and I exchanged frequent emails. In one of the notes, she mentioned seeing a new tabby cat that dropped by one day to eat. Christina believed this new grey tabby to be a male. The new cat continued to dine with the other kitties, and over the next few days, I received more emails about his situation. Christina was concerned for the health of this new cat. Each note was filled with new details and the description more troubling than the prior.

It seemed as if he was having a difficult time eating. He appeared to have trouble chewing and swallowing the food. Christina then recalled that upon her first sighting of our new guest, she noticed he was squinting. This indicated to Christina that in spite of her initial doubt about correctly assessing his eye condition, she was now 100% certain there was a problem with his eyes. Christina wondered if he had an eye infection or eye injury.

The last note in the series said that the cat "was shaking." She expressed her deep concern for the kitty and asked if I could assist in getting medical care for him. I shared her concern and could feel her heartfelt compassion. I didn't tell her how seriously concerned I was for the sick cat, as I didn't want to further alarm her. The truth is I had a knot in the pit of my stomach. I felt we had a seriously ill or injured cat on our hands.

I agreed that our new charge needed medical attention and pronto. I called Dr. Mixon's office to put them on standby for scheduling a check-up and neuter appointment for the little guy. As always, they were kind, and at the ready to accommodate me and my newest feral feline. The first order of business was to trap him as quickly as possible. I decided to "bring out the big guns" to ensure a successful trapping. This was no time for one of my hit-or-miss trapping excursions.

Again, I enlisted the help of master trapper Chris and his "trap of last resort" drop trap. I sent an urgent email to Chris with a plea for help to trap a sick kitty. He immediately responded, and we made plans to trap that very day.

I asked Christina to go and see if our tabby was present. She assured me he was there, in his usual spot along the fenceline and appearing very sedated. I asked her to talk to him in a very soft voice to let him know that he would be fed. I was worried that he would wander off before Chris and I arrived. Christina met us at the colony to assist with the trapping. It was time for the daily feeding, so her role was to call the cats to dinner. I have taken to calling her "the cat whisperer." She's gained the trust of the cats and formed relationships with them in an astonishing short amount of time. True to form, Daddy was the first to come to the table. His family followed and they all ate their fill.

Then I saw the new tabby. He was nestled in his usual spot along the fence and watching the activity. I remember thinking it seemed as if he was trying to appear inconspicuous. If so, he was doing a right good job of that. With the combination of his brown tabby fur against the weathered brown fence, the contour of his body almost seemed at one with the fence. Just as Christina had described his eating ritual to me, he patiently waited for all the cats to eat before he approached the baited trap. He was an easy catch.

The procedure with the drop trap is to transfer the cat from the larger drop trap to a conventional trap for transport. The conventional trap is positioned against one end of the drop trap and the doors of both traps are opened creating a narrow passageway for the cat to move from the larger trap to the conventional trap. The cats, afraid and stressed after being trapped, frantically run the very short distance from the drop trap into the transport trap.

Chris and I were mortified when the tabby cat

slammed his nose very hard against the conventional trap during the transfer process. The poor little guy couldn't put his brakes on fast enough to avoid crashing into the back of the trap. He surely didn't need any further medical complications.

I took our new feral feline to Doctor Mike bright and early the next morning. I asked them to first test him for feline aids and leukemia before proceeding with the exam and neuter procedure. Cats that are positive for these two diseases shouldn't live among cats that aren't vaccinated. I prayed that he would be free of disease, and, thankfully, he was.

Or should I say "she". When the technician called me with the test results, she mentioned that the kitty was a female. I had registered the tabby as "Jake" that morning; I giggled and told her, "Well, in that case, change Jake's name to Jackie."

An associate of Dr. Mike's called me a short time after to give me her initial report. The examination revealed that Jackie weighed just five pounds and was about nine months old. She was not pregnant. That was comforting news. She had numerous and significant fight wounds and bruises about her face, head, and all over her body. The wounds were of various ages and at varying stages of healing. The injuries had caused her face to swell, including the area around her eyes. This was the cause of her squinting and difficulty with eating. The doctor said that Jackie was most certainly in pain from the wounds around her face and head.

Dr. Stribley advised me they would clip around her wounds, treat them, and administer an antibiotic by injection to stave off infection. She would also need a shot of pain medication. She recommended Jackie receive antibiotics by mouth for seven days. I had already envisioned I would need to foster her beyond the standard forty-eight hour post-spay protocol.

We agreed they would compound the medication with tuna flavoring so I could mix it with canned food. I asked Dr. Stribley how Jackie behaved during the process. I mentioned that she was a newcomer to the colony and we weren't sure if she was feral or a stray. Dr. Stribley described that Jackie was timid, fearful, and cowered at the back of her cage throughout the day. She allowed them to lightly touch her side. I asked the doctor if they thought she was feral or a stray, but Dr. Stribley said she didn't have enough time with Jackie to make that assessment.

I guessed that Jackie sustained these injuries trying to fend off males wanting to mate with her. She may have also been attacked by cats protecting their colony from the intrusion of new cats. I was filled with compassion for Jackie after hearing that the bruises and bites had caused her face to swell. It never would have occurred to me that an animal's facial injuries could result in facial swelling and impaired vision.

I then had an "aha moment." I remembered the photos of the pop celebrity singer Rihanna who made the news after receiving a severe beating about her head and face from her then-boyfriend. Her face was swollen almost beyond recognition and her eyes were nearly swollen shut. I imagined that her vision would have been severely limited and restricted to squinting.

I compared that to what Jackie must have endured. My heart went out to her. I shed some tears thinking about the suffering she'd already experienced. For such a young cat, she had undergone more than her share of adversity.

Jackie progressed well during her convalescence at my home. I, too, saw the timid behavior that Dr. Stribley had described. This explained Christina's observation of Jackie waiting to eat until after all the other cats had finished. I now understood it was her choice to eat last and alone. She hadn't fared well in fights with other cats, and those experiences contributed to her timidity.

I was happy that the injuries didn't lessen her appetite. She ate and slept well. I figured out by the end of the third day that she was definitely a feral cat. She never came to the front of the cage, choosing instead to remain at the back, which is standard feral cat behavior. Coming to the front of the cage is a social behavior exhibited by stray and owned cats.

Another behavior that confirmed her feral status was her rather impassioned hiss when I reached a little too far into the cage to remove some soiled newspaper. She enjoyed using her litter box as her bed. I've learned that using the litter box as a bed is an almost universal trait of ferals. They seek the security of the box in preference to the open space of the crate. This behavior is identical to that of their socialized cousins who seek out boxes, bags, cat beds, and any other container they can manage to squeeze into.

By the end of the week, Jackie was no longer squinting, which confirmed to me that she was healing. I was relieved to see her progress, and thankful she had this quiet time away from the colony where she could heal and rest. This foster stay also provided a safe refuge for recovery without the threat of attacks from other animals.

When I released Jackie back to her home, it was a smooth exit; she wasn't reluctant to vacate the cage like our little Sally. She was out and gone in nanoseconds. I reported the successful release to Christina and asked her to keep me updated on Jackie's continued status in the colony.

I'm saddened to write that we never saw Jackie again. I believe that when she ran out of that crate, she just kept running. Christina and I remain deeply affected by her loss. After all, she'd only recently found us. I've thought a lot about her, and I wonder how she is faring out there in the wild. Is someone feeding her? Is she healthy? Is she safe? Has she been attacked by any more cats?

Her unique circumstances presented some

challenges to successfully returning cats to the colony. Jackie was new to the pride and not an established family member. I believe her timidity made it difficult for her to form relationships with the other cats. Her assimilation into the group was further compromised by her health issues. Probably if she had, upon her return, encountered just one cat she felt connected to, she would have remained.

I mentioned to Chris that Jackie had run away and how distressed I was feeling. He said he has also had cats go missing, and advised me that she may be back. Christina remains on the lookout for Jackie, and we hope that one day soon she will return to us.

PART TWO
My Rescued Cats

"HALEY"

"Samantha"

"PRINCESS"

Chapter 6
HOW IT BEGAN: THE DUAL RESCUE

My first encounter with Princess was memorable for a couple of reasons. It was my first visit home to San Antonio since my father had died a few months earlier, and everything felt different. But the experience of meeting Princess was mostly notable because it was unlike any of my usual, warm introductions to a new cat. This initiation instead set a new record for contentious cat encounters.

As I reached down to pet her, I remember thinking that she was the most beautiful cat I'd ever seen. I couldn't have known that Princess subscribed to the old adage, "look but don't touch." She greeted me with a huge, emphatic hiss and followed up with a snarl, just to make sure I got the message.

Oh yes! Message received, loud and clear. It pained me that this gorgeous creature wouldn't allow me to touch her. Not wanting to increase her agitation, I withdrew my hand and stepped away. Princess was a silver-shaded Chinchilla with trademark white and silver markings. She had huge, saucer-shaped blue eyes, and her back legs were skirted with long, luxurious fur.

One of my friends saw her walking from behind and commented that it looked as if she was wearing pantaloons. Princess was a dead ringer for the feline eating from the crystal bowl in the Tasty Feast cat food commercials.

Princess's mistress was my mom, and Mother quickly came to her defense when I received what came to be a signature, hostile greeting from the feline. "Oh, she's a little shy around strangers is all," Mom explained.

Oh, really! That's not how I would describe a shy cat. I quickly learned that mother's depiction of the cat's behavior was actually code for "she's a one-woman cat. Don't even think about befriending her."

My siblings and I often joked behind Mother's

back about the beautiful but untouchable Princess. I distinctly remember tossing around the term "Princess of Darkness" more than a few times. The fussy feline was completely devoted to my mom. She almost never left my mother's line of sight. Mom loved to tell how Princess would accompany her to the bathroom at all hours of the night.

I'm still mystified by the vision of Princess leaving her comfortable bed to escort my mom to the bathroom several times a night. Mind you, I believe my cats love me to the fullest, feline extent possible, but I wouldn't wager any bets that any of them would interrupt their sleep to walk me to the bathroom.

Princess had the most contact with my brother, Lionel. He lived in town and visited Mom often. Common reasoning would suggest that the feline would have developed some measure of a relationship with him, but common sense would be wrong.

On one of my trips home to visit Mom, Lionel came over and encountered Princess in the living room. He bent down to greet her and asked, "Girl, do you remember me?" She responded with her trademark exaggerated hiss. "Yep, she remembers me," he replied. The three of us siblings still laugh about that as if it occurred yesterday.

Princess was an enigma. Her love for my mom was obvious, but we were puzzled by her frequent biting behavior. A calm petting session would, for no apparent reason, turn ugly with Princess biting Mom on her hands and arms. The ever-faithful defender of her beloved cat, Mom minimized the situation by calling them "love bites." But in reality the bites were no laughing matter. Mother frequently had bite marks extending from her hands to her elbows.

Mom's staunch defense of Princess was due to the fact that this gorgeous creature saved her life. No, the cat didn't save Mother from a burning building or perform any other kind of physical gallantry. Princess helped promote emotional healing for her mistress by lifting Mom out of the depths of profound grief, anxiety, and panic that developed after my father died.

Mom found herself living alone for the first time in her life.

When Mom was a young woman, social mores dictated that respectable, single girls didn't live on their own. Growing up in a Hispanic household in Galveston, Texas, she followed the cultural custom of moving directly from her father's home to her husband's home.

While Mom and Dad lived with pets most of their lives, they chose to be petless the last few years of Dad's life as they traversed the country in their luxury travel trailer. We three kids were blindsided that Mom would experience such intense emotional upheaval to living alone. The loneliness was immediate and severe.

Soon after Dad's death, Mom experienced her first

panic attack while out running errands. She described it to me as a crippling fear that seized her and wouldn't let her go. She was driving during the first incident, and, fearing she would crash the car, she pulled off the road to wait for the panic to subside. A few minutes later, heart still racing, she resumed the familiar route back to her house. The panic was exacerbated by disorientation as she desperately tried to get home.

Such panic attacks continued a few more times before we were able to convince her to see her doctor. He recommended anti-anxiety medication to help ease her into her new life of living alone. I recommended an additional prescription: I suggested she adopt a cat.

I reminded her how much she loved cats, and I ascribed that my life as a single woman was enriched by the companionship of my cats. I advised her that simply having another living being in the house would make her feel less alone. The responsibility of caring for the cat would give her a reason to get up in the morning. I explained to her she needed to be needed as much as she needed to love and be loved. I all but guaranteed that her loneliness and anxiety would dissipate with the adoption of a cat. I remember telling myself I hoped I hadn't oversold the benefits of life with a cat!

Mom said she would think about it. A few days later, I received a call from a very giddy mom! I'll never forget her opening words: "Oh Janet, I have found an angel."

I listened for fifteen minutes as Mom described the beautiful, blue-eyed kitten she'd christened Princess. Mom's panic attacks stopped instantly, and she soon discontinued all the medication. Mother often referred to Princess as her "guardian angel", and she shared five very happy years with Princess before succumbing to stomach cancer.

As Mom was in the last stages of the disease, she asked me the one, big question I was dreading. Would I consider adopting Princess after she died? Mother explained that of her three children, I was the most logical choice. My sister had a cat and a dog, and she didn't think my single brother could commit to the responsibility of pet ownership. Mom said that she knew how hard I had taken the death of my beloved Persian a few years earlier, and she worried that I may not be emotionally ready to adopt another cat. The truth is, I was ready to adopt another cat—just not that cat. I told Mom I wanted think about it.

I considered what would happen to Princess if I declined to take her. It was clear she wouldn't be going with either of my siblings. The only other alternative would be to surrender the feline to an animal shelter. This wouldn't have provided the happily-ever-after "forever home" for this kitty that was so important to my mother.

Her celebrity looks would have attracted many

prospective guardians, but her customary hostile greeting to strangers would have frightened away most of her prospects. Even if she was lucky enough to be adopted, a new caregiver would soon tire of the surly attitude and return the feline for untenable behavior. Princess would have been caught up in a revolving door of failed adoptions, destined to live out her life as a shelter animal.

I had to consider the larger issue, of wanting to fulfill my mother's only deathbed request. I couldn't refuse her wish, nor subject her beloved kitty to a life of uncertainty and a possible lifetime sentence in a shelter—or worse. I decided to accept the challenge and my decision brought Mom a lot of peace.

As the cancer progressed, I shared caretaker responsibilities with my sister and spent many days and nights at Mom's home. Princess sensed that Mom was too weak to interact with her, and she changed her nighttime routine from sleeping on Mom's bed to sleeping at the edge of my bed. Gee, was the Ice Princess starting to thaw? I was happy for the change in attitude, though, and Princess slowly began to allow me to pet her in brief increments.

The snarling and hissing ceased altogether, but the random biting continued. Over time, I was able to decrease the biting by 90% by firmly saying "no" and walking away from her.

Years later, I learned about the widely-held theory behind what causes cats to engage in random biting. The phenomenon is called "petting induced aggression", and it happens when the cat becomes over-stimulated. Cats that are declawed like Princess react with the only means they have to express their displeasure, and that's with their teeth. Cats exhibit subtle behavioral signs that they are approaching over-stimulation, and savvy owners can prevent an incident by immediately halting the petting session.

After Mom died, Princess embarked on her maiden road trip with me down Interstate Highway 10 West to Houston. I was surprised by her rapid adjustment to life without my mom. Her relationship with me was of course different than the one she'd forged with Mother. I didn't need her in the ways that Mom did.

We quickly negotiated our own special rituals. She demonstrated her affection for me in ways that were new to me as a cat guardian. She frequently nudged me with her head, as if to say, *"Hey, I'm saying hello here. Are you going to acknowledge me or what?"*

Other times, when we were in the same room and she caught me looking at her, she would leave her roosting place, walk over and lie down beside me. I would tell her, "Princess, I wasn't calling you. You didn't need to move."

She loved going out on our enclosed patio. Mom hadn't allowed her to explore the great outdoors, so this presented a huge quality of life enhancement. I taught her to walk on a leash and she loved peering into the downstairs windows of neighboring homes to glimpse a cat or dog. She became the curiosity of the small neighborhood as drivers stopped to do a double take.

They would often circle back, roll down their windows, and tell me they'd never seen someone walk a cat.

All of my friends thought Princess was gorgeous, but she wouldn't allow anyone else to touch her. I explained her behavior by saying she was a "one-woman cat." Princess never accompanied me to the bathroom at night. That was a sacred ritual that she bestowed only on my mom.

Princess rescued my mom from the profound grief she experienced as a new widow. My decision to adopt Princess was a rescue in return, because it saved her from the shelter, where she wouldn't have fared well. I never regretted my decision, because Mom deserved peace, and Princess deserved to be rewarded with a second chance at a happy life.

Princess' life with me as my only Persian child lasted twelve months, until the arrival of kittens Rory and Samantha, Persian male and female siblings. Rory and Samantha were the offspring of papa cat Samson and mama cat Delilah, who lived with my neighbor, Judy. Rory was caramel-colored with orange eyes, and Samantha was black and silver with golden-orange eyes. She had a small overbite, which made her all the more endearing. I once teased Judy that she'd sold me a defective cat!

One of the siblings' favorite games was to chase the ball from the top of the stairs down to the first floor. Over and over, they would race up the stairs, wait for me to toss them the ball, then charge down the steps as fast as their short little Persian legs could carry them. Their sibling antics of wrestling and kickboxing kept me entertained for hours.

Princess, on the other hand, was not amused. She saw them as irritating interlopers encroaching on her territory. That sacred territory included her physical space and ownership of me. I remember my sister asking me how Princess was adjusting to the new additions. She and my brother were deeply concerned, anticipating conflict if not an all-out war! I laughed wryly, confirming their worst fears. "It's not going well at all. She wants them gone."

Princess reacted to her step-siblings by isolating herself from them. Since Rory and Sam followed me around the house all their waking hours, this meant that Princess's time with me was severely compromised. I hated that Princess spent so much time alone, though. There was no way to see her other than to close the kittens in a room by themselves.

Princess soon grew tired of the self-imposed, solitary confinement, and after a few weeks, she made an about face. After that, she remained in the same room with me and the babies. Although she never befriended them, she tolerated them, and that's all I asked of her.

Samantha was a true "Mama's girl." She relished one-on-one time with me. While I sat in my bedroom chair to read, Sam happily perched on the lamp table beside me. I didn't realize how spoiled she was, until I shared a perplexing situation with my coworkers. Samantha started waking up in the middle of the night with loud, prolonged wailing.

I worried that she had suddenly fallen ill and got of bed to investigate. After establishing that she wasn't sick, I spoke soothingly to her, and within minutes the crying subsided. She then signaled a desire for a rousing game of fetch. This series of events went on for three consecutive nights.

The telling of the story elicited raucous laughter from my colleagues, and I then realized I had been played! Samantha's nocturnal shenanigans were clearly a well-thought-out ploy to engage me in a nighttime playdate. The behavior stopped after I ceased getting out of bed.

After I moved back to San Antonio, three cats in tow, a situation with my feral cats made me decide to seek consultation from internationally recognized animal communicator, Sonya Fitzpatrick, which you read about in an earlier story.

Sonya communicates with living and deceased animals telepathically. She tunes in to the animals after seeing their photo, seeing them in person, or speaking by phone or face to face with the animal's human.

Sonya spoke with the feral cat about the issues at hand, and then my resident cats each took a turn sharing with her. In setting up the appointment, I requested that Sonya communicate with the feral cat and emailed a photo of the cat.

I didn't mention that I lived with other cats, nor did I request a consultation with the cats that shared my home. Princess took the lead and was the first to communicate with Sonya. Princess announced herself to Sonya as "the most beautiful cat in the household."

Sonya described the kitty as having silver/white fur and large, round blue eyes. *Yep,* I laughed to myself, *that feline is most definitely the Princess.*

Princess had one major concern to discuss with Sonya: "Will Mom be bringing home any more cats?"

It was a funny if not prudent inquiry. Princess had gone from being an only child to being part of a multi-cat household with four step-siblings. In addition, she had to contend with the feral cats I fostered as they recovered from spay/neuter surgery. Rory told Sonya he liked that each cat had his/her own placemat under the food dish, and Samantha mentioned she liked the tree next to her bowl. She referred to the artificial silk tree as "her tree."

Sam also commented she felt I was very fair and loved each of them the same. Those words provided great comfort to me, because as the mistress of the household, I often worried whether I was giving each cat equal doses of my attention.

The biggest surprise of the consultation was the participation of my first Persian, named Pasha, who'd passed away some ten years earlier. Pasha said that he wanted to quickly pop in and convey that he appreciated how much I loved him. I was so overwhelmed by his unexpected attendance that all I could do was sob! I regret that I was unable to pull myself together to convey a message back to him.

Pasha shared my home for nine short years before succumbing to kidney disease. I named Pasha for a unique shop in my Houston neighborhood called Pasha Imports. The term Pasha is an ancient Turkish term for a high ranking military or political figure. My Pasha was indeed regal looking, and the name suited him purrfectly.

He was a black smoke Persian, with the trademark white undercoat, silver/black top coat, and amber-colored eyes. He was my steadfast companion and travel buddy. We made numerous trips to San Antonio, and he relished the car travel. I taught him to be comfortable riding in a car by taking him on short stints around the neighborhood as a kitten. He even used the litterbox while the car was moving during our three-hour road trips. This kitty was so adaptable that I often said for Pasha, "Home is where his litterbox happens to be."

My parents had a nickname for their grandcat—Pashito, meaning Little Pasha in Spanish. Pasha garnered special attention from everyone who met him, making a lasting impression on his legion of fans. My friend Mary Leigh named her new cat after Pasha and my Aunt Lucy called him "the Little Owl", due to his prominent golden peepers.

At times the adoration people felt for Pasha left me feeling a bit neglected. My parent's telephone calls to me always began with, "How's Pasha?" I'll never forget the reaction from friends and family after Pasha and I were involved in a car accident. Yep, you guessed it. The first question everyone asked was, "Is Pasha OK?"

The kitty was so laid back that he frequently took short naps in the exam rooms at veterinarian offices. Clinic staff commented that they had never seen a cat as easygoing as Pasha. He loved people, the more the merrier. He routinely attended my parties, and would position himself in the area of the room for maximum human interaction. Upon observing Pasha's party persona, one of my male friends jokingly asked me, "Is your cat on drugs?"

One time my parents and some friends were visiting me at my home in Houston. Pasha was lying on top of the television set, snoozing away, one of his favorite spots to slumber. About forty-five minutes into the visit, Pasha got up to stretch. The female guest immediately belted out a blood-curdling scream. Upon catching her breath, she divulged that she'd noticed a cat on top of the television set, but assumed it was a stuffed animal because it never moved a muscle!

I added two stray cats to my trio of Persians after returning to San Antonio, and my life as a rescuer was born. I soon had "blended" my family of designer cats with alley cats! I started a nighttime routine of saying goodnight to the cats before going to sleep.

The first evening my boyfriend John spent at my home was the first time anyone other than the cats had experienced my nightly ritual. After turning out the bedside lamp, I began the recitation of cat names: "Good night Princess, good night Samantha, good night Rory . . ."

About this time, John interrupted me with a wry, "So what is this, The Waltons?"

Once we both stopped laughing, I explained that I hadn't considered the origins of this practice, but as a self-proclaimed Waltons junkie, I acknowledged borrowing my "Waltons goodnight" from the program. If you're too young to know or too old to remember, the Waltons was a weekly television drama from the 1970s that followed the struggles of a large, three generation Virginia family from the Depression through World War II. Each segment ended at bedtime with members of the family saying goodnight by calling out each other's names from their respective bedrooms. With seven children, two parents, and two grandparents participating in the ritual, it was an endearing and dramatic conclusion to the weekly program.

I will always cherish the memories of my four

"designer cats." Princess lived thirteen years with me after Mom's death and passed away at the ripe old age of eighteen. Rory and Samantha died within a year of each other, just before their fifteenth and sixteenth birthdays. Pasha died of kidney disease after only nine short years.

"PASHA"

"KELLY"

Chapter 7
LA HIJA BONITA

Each time I travel, like most pet guardians, I worry about the well-being of my cats while I'm away. I especially fret over how they will behave toward each other. Will the fur fly in mommy's absence? Will I return home to a "cat-astrophe" of broken lamps and furniture?

If my cat Kelly could talk, this is what she would

have told me after I returned from a recent four day trip: *"Mommy, mommy, mommy, come here quickly. I want to tell you what happened while you were gone. The other cats misbehaved. Joey was a very bad boy. He broke your blue vase. He wouldn't leave Haley alone. He spilled his food and water. Rory peed outside the litter box, but he didn't mean to. Carrie Ann knocked the pillows off the kitchen chair and the bench in the living room. She disobeyed you and played with the mini blind cords in the kitchen. But I was a very good girl."*

If you didn't realize it by now, Kelly is our resident tattletale! She's the most possessive of my three females and the eldest girl. She also holds the title of drama queen. I can always count on her to overreact to even a minor infraction from one of the other kitties. When feeling threatened, she will ramp up from a growl to a bloodcurdling scream in less than five seconds. If I didn't know better, I would think she was being ripped apart by a wild animal. What precipitates this response? It can be anything, even something as minor as the offending cat simply walking by at a distance she perceives as too close, or staring at her for too long.

Kelly has added another designation to her resume—that of disciplinarian. She has recently taken to scolding Joey when she hears me telling him to stop clawing the furniture. She paces back and forth in front of him, screeching at him in a very loud and annoyed tone. It is one of her funniest and cutest antics. I have heard of other females taking on the role of disciplinarian in a multiple cat household, too. My friend Judy has described how her mother cat still corrected her adult "kittens" with a scolding meow, sometimes followed by a thump to the side of the head.

Kelly is very intelligent. I know that everyone thinks their animals are the smartest pets to ever walk the earth, but this feline is the real deal. Kelly frequently follows me into my walk-in pantry. My cats don't wear collars with bells, so I can't hear them as they move around the house. Kelly gets accidentally trapped in the pantry at least a couple of times per month—she must interpret walk-in to mean she is invited to walk in at any time.

I often wonder how, even after ten years, she still manages to sneak in behind me. It's quite befuddling. One morning while making breakfast, I opened the pantry door to find Kelly in there. She'd sneaked in the evening before and spent the entire night in there! On the floor of the pantry, there was about a 2' x 2' area of kitty litter. Some of the litter looked wet. I realized that overnight Kelly felt a need to urinate. She smelled the unopened bag of kitty litter on the floor and scratched a hole in it large enough to spill some onto the floor. This incident still ranks as one of the best examples of cat intelligence I've ever witnessed.

Kelly came into my life at the persistence of my neighbors. The boys—ages six, eight, and ten—

motioned to me one day as I was getting out of my car, "Janet, have you seen the kitten in your bushes?" I didn't investigate that day, as there were already three cats in the household who proudly claimed me as their human. I didn't want to be tempted to enlarge the family.

A few days later, the children summoned me again. "There's a kitten in your yard, come see."

This time, I gave in and went to see the brown tabby kitten. It seems the boys had already decided this feline's fate, and her fate was to be with me.

"Are you going to keep her?"

"No, boys, I am not going to keep her."

Try as I might, though, I wasn't able to forget about the stray tabby kitten. She wasn't one of the most beautiful cats I had ever seen; she was petite with a decidedly cute face, green eyes, and lots of orange coloring.

I would later find out that the boys had tricked me. Kelly wasn't a stray, and they darn well knew it. Later that week, I was driving up my street and saw the stray kitten in someone's else's front yard. It was typical February weather for San Antonio—cold and rainy, with nighttime temperatures plunging into the 20's. It concerned me that this kitten was, literally and figuratively, out in the cold.

Without giving it much thought, I pulled over, scooped her up, and put her in my car. As I was driving home, I thought, now what the heck am I going to do with this stray feline? I decided I wouldn't worry about the lack of a long-term plan. My immediate goal was to get her off the streets and out of the cold.

My other three cats, all Persians—two females and one male—didn't seem to mind Kelly too much, so I thought I would consider keeping her. I told myself again not to worry about the absence of a plan, and to focus on the good deed I'd done by getting her out of harm's way.

Two mornings later, at 7:15 a.m., there was a knock at my front door. I was getting ready for work and wondered who could be calling at that hour. I answered the door to find a woman looking none too happy and accompanied by a school-aged boy. The woman introduced herself and immediately announced, "You stole our kitten. Our son has been crying his eyes out, just crying his eyes out since you took her."

Gee, I thought to myself, *nice to meet you, too. And by the way, nothing like being put on the defensive in the sacred domain of my own home.*

As if to add insult to injury, this inquisition occurred before my second cup of coffee, never a wise decision. I always think better after a second cup.

The previous day, I'd confided to a neighbor about nabbing the kitten and bringing her home. My neighbor was acquainted with Kelly and had plenty to say. "Oh, that's Koli. She lives next door. But listen, I wouldn't mind at all if you adopted her, because they're mean to her. They have a dog and another cat that live inside, and they make Koli stay outside all the time, even in this freezing weather. I promise I won't say anything to them."

I remembered her reassurance after I was accused of stealing the cat. *Yes, of course you won't say anything. This will be our secret. Really? Why the heck did you rat me out, then?*

Koli's owner divulged that Koli had been banished to the outdoors by her husband because she wouldn't stop climbing the curtains. The woman explained that "Koli just loves being outside."

It was then that the discussion got a little heated. I told her rather unabashedly, "That is very interesting news to me, because since she's been here, she hasn't once asked to go outside. Furthermore, I don't believe it's safe for cats to live outside. They're at risk of disease and injury from other animals, pregnancy, and being run over by a car." *Hey,* I told myself, *if you can put me on the defensive in my own home, I can give it right back.*

(In telling this part of the story to one of my male friends, he interrupted me to laughingly ask, "I just want to know, were the police called out?" I think it disappointed him to hear that thankfully, no, the drama didn't escalate into a police matter.)

The woman then asked if I would be home that evening so she could return with her husband. *Oh goody,* I thought, *round two with the queen of rudeness and her mean-to-cats husband.* She said they would determine as a family whether Koli would be better off with them or with me.

Wow! She surprised me with this declaration. She decidedly changed her tune, thinking that perhaps they had enough of this troublemaking little furball. I told my sister about the ugly incident, and she had a visceral reaction to the kitten's name. "Can we please ditch the name Koli?" she pleaded. "Is that like Ko Lee or E- Coli? Who the heck names a cat after a disease?"

As threatened, the whole family darkened my doorstep at seven that evening. Dad, mom, and their seven-year-old son came a calling. Oh, joy! The woman said that her son wanted to see Koli. I led them to the kitchen, and Koli promptly ran away from the boy and his parents. She positioned herself as far under the table and out of reach as she could get.

Well, I thought, *no love lost there. Why am I not surprised?*

The mom then explained that after much consideration, they determined that I would be allowed to keep the cat. She was much too destructive. They asked if the boy could have visiting privileges. I said yes without blinking an eye, because I knew the odds of him following through on it were slim. And he never did.

The only thing missing from this tale is the explanation of how I came to realize the neighbor boys were trying to deceive me into believing that

Kelly was a stray. After meeting Kelly's previous family, I learned the neighbor kids go to school with the little boy. So they were very much aware of the neglectful treatment of Kelly, and correctly assumed that she would be much better off with me. This family owns two cats. They love and spoil them—as they deserve—and they are full-fledged members of their family.

Kelly is living happily-ever-after with me, and she was my first "rescue." I use that term loosely, since she was not a homeless cat when I "stole her." Perhaps the rescue term fits since I rescued her from a neglectful environment. And oh, what a special girl she is! Kelly is my garden cat, loving to chase butterflies and birds as she keeps me company while I perform the perfunctory tasks of weeding and pruning. I have never co-habitated with such a multi-talented cat. She surely wears the title of biggest character.

For example, she has recently taught herself to sing. I thought it was a coincidence the first time she started meowing loudly while I was singing. The second and third times she chimed in, I knew she was trying to harmonize with me. Well, not so much harmonizing as loudly wailing, but you get the picture! My little girl can sing . . . I'm such a proud mama. And, to top things off, she simultaneously climbs up my leg while belting out a tune. Maybe one day we will perform on the Dave Letterman Show.

There is one last Kelly accomplishment that bears

bragging about: I am teaching her Spanish. After all, we do live in San Antonio, where fifty percent of the population speaks Spanish. She has learned "gato" (cat), "bonita" (pretty) and "hija" (daughter). I give all my cats nicknames, and usually more than one. Kelly has four other names, and she's learned them all. She answers to Kelly Girl, Kellita, Kellyrita and Hija Bonita. In fact, she comes running from across the house when I call out "Hija Bonita". She purrs when I call her by her alternate names.

I feel incredibly blessed to have Kelly in my life. She's a wonderful and loyal companion. I would have never guessed that this little plain Jane would turn out to be hands down the most intelligent cat that has ever owned me. She shows me every day how much she appreciates being removed from her previous family. She sleeps on my bed every night, and follows me around the house, much like dogs do with their family members. Kelly lets me know when she needs some private time with me. She meows at me to follow her to another room, and I'm forced to oblige her for some one-on-one mommy time. You won't see me complaining about it!

"TYLER"

Chapter 8

MY WALMART GREETER

T yler was my Walmart Greeter, meeting everyone just inside the front door with a smile and a hello. One of my favorite Tyler stories comes from the time two plumbers arrived to do some work on my house, and Tyler greeted them with his usual "how do you do" meow. The two men ignored him and walked past, so Tyler meowed again. They continued their silent stride through the room, and I could see Tyler thinking *Hey, what's a cat gotta do around here to get noticed? Let's try another meow.*

Feeling like the protective mama, I told the guys, "Excuse me, but here's the thing: he's waiting for you to acknowledge him, you know, with a hello. Sorry to say that he will keep meowing at you until you say hello back."

The two muy-macho plumbers looked at me like I was more than a little crazy. They nervously mumbled a greeting to Tyler, then looked back at me again to see if that was good enough. I just smiled and nodded.

Tyler always accompanied me to answer the front door. The moment he saw me heading that direction, he would run ahead of me to get there first. How he loved company! This kitty never knew a stranger, and wanted to be part of whatever venture brought new friends into his life. This meant Mommy had to supervise Tyler's interaction with the various contract workers that visited our home. I had to prevent him from standing too close to electrical parts, tool bags, and whatever supplies the workers brought with them.

Tyler was my steadfast companion for nine years, and it would be safer to say he found me than the other way around. My sister and nephew were visiting me in the kitchen one day, when we heard very loud wailing coming from outside. We opened the door to see a pitifully thin black and white cat with gorgeous green eyes on the stoop, like he came calling every day.

He was so thin that the sides of his stomach were concave, yet he was still handsome. It was obvious he was starving. I gave him some food and his behavior stunned us all. He would eat a few bites, rush over to nuzzle my leg, return to the bowl, then come back to me, for a good five minutes. We couldn't believe that an obviously starving cat would interrupt his meal with such immediate and repetitive gratitude. I have never seen it since.

For the next ten days, I fed Tyler on and off. He didn't come to the house every day, so I asked the neighbors on both sides of me if they knew if the kitty belonged to anyone. One of the neighbors said the people next to them were taking care of Tyler, and he was living under their deck. The living-under-the deck part did not sit well with me. A few more days passed, and he returned begging for food. I was horrified to see a large fleshy wound on one of his hind legs. I asked the neighbors if the other folks had, in fact, adopted Tyler.

No, it seems, they had not. They had too much going on with the new baby.

I knew what that meant. Now that the stray kitty needed a doctor and would require more expense beyond daily feeding, they had decided not to adopt him.

I took him to my wonderful veterinarian, and he

said the wound would have soon become infected without attention. Given the position and depth of the wound, Dr. Mixon thought that Tyler had probably been hit by a car. He treated the wound, bandaged it, and sent us on our way with the required medications and the "dreaded collar," the cone-shaped plastic collar that fits around the animal's neck to ensure that the bandages are not chewed off.

At this point I realized I'd made the decision to adopt him myself, so I named him Tyler, after a friend's adorable three-year-old boy. I remember thinking I needed a really cute name for a really cute cat, and "Tyler" fit the bill, purrfectly.

Tyler was a party animal. He never missed a social gathering, greeting each guest individually like the perfect host before plopping himself down in the center of the action. He enjoyed festivities of all kinds—holiday affairs, dinner parties, and mom's girlfriend gatherings.

When I had a boyfriend over for dinner, Tyler was my able co-host. Tyler was much-loved by all my male friends and relatives. If there was a cat equivalent to the expression, "he's a man's man," it would fit Tyler. He always won the men over with his gregarious and relaxed personality. He also endeared himself to my male friends because he was a large, strapping kitty. As a result of the regular and bountiful meals he now enjoyed, he'd filled out to a healthy 13 pounds.

Whenever anyone inferred he was getting a little

hefty, I would correct them and say, "We prefer the term big-boned."

Tyler must have been starved for quite some time when he adopted me. I believe he retained a memory of being starved as a stray and this prevented him from feeling secure that he would always have enough to eat. His feeding routine was to quickly clean his bowl, then to scavenge what he could from the other cats' leftovers.

I didn't think Tyler could purr for the first two years he lived with me. I thought it was kind of strange that he never purred, but I didn't make too much of it. I decided his magnetic personality and other sterling qualities made up for his lack of purring. Then one day during a petting session, I heard a very faint purr.

Wow, I thought to myself! We have a breakthrough. I grabbed him and kissed him, saying: "You can purr!" I then realized Tyler had been purring all along. I'd simply not heard his soft, gentle purr. I was accustomed to my household of very loud purrers. After Tyler taught me how to listen to his quiet purr, I enjoyed his melodic purring every day from that moment on.

I told Tyler's rescue story to a few of my cat-loving friends. To my surprise, two of them volunteered to help me with the veterinarian bills. In addition to the wound treatment, he would need to be neutered and get the rest of his shots, so I gratefully accepted the help.

Tyler would prove to be an easy patient. Even though he was a new member of the family, he readily trusted me. I believe he understood I was trying to help him, and his compliance was a display of gratitude. He tolerated wearing that darn collar and twice-daily dressing changes for two weeks without so much as a single hiss.

Tyler was so grateful to have a home that he was always unassuming with my other four cats. He and Kelly became fast friends and enjoyed frequent mutual grooming and wrestling sessions.

Kelly taught Tyler to enjoy gardening with Mom, so he became my second garden cat. He loved to lounge in the yard at sunset and into the evening. Sometimes he was an errant child and would stay out past curfew, which was 9:00 p.m. on weekdays and 10:00 p.m. on weekends.

He busted curfew a few times and kept me up worrying about him past 11:00 p.m. on a weekday. That brat cat! He never left the yard during those late night outings, though, to my knowledge, and I was very thankful for that. He stayed in the back yard and hid from me as I called out his name over and over. Favorite hiding spots were under the deck where Mommy couldn't go in after him, or under the pampas grass. I always wondered if he somehow knew that I was allergic to the pampas; this hiding place provided a safe haven before he finally relented to coming inside to bed.

Kelly and I were singing our loud duet one day when, lo and behold, Tyler joined in. Who knew the feline could sing? I use the term "sing" rather loosely, of course. You see, it was very, very bad cat singing—hilariously bad. He didn't have Kelly's timing by any stretch of the imagination, because she sang steadily throughout the song. Tyler, on the other hand, chimed in about every 5-10 notes. His efforts reminded me of a backup singer coming in late for his part every time and ruining the entire ensemble.

Ok, so music was not his thing. He more than made up for it with enthusiasm and adorableness.

I would lose my darling Tyler to feline leukemia. His loss is still very painful. All cat guardians need to immunize their kitties against this terminal disease. Since he was primarily an indoor cat, it never crossed my mind that his limited backyard jaunts would expose him to this incurable disease.

I've often wondered if he could have become infected by a stray during one of his past bedtime excursions. It wasn't until the end of his life that I realized he'd also been the "Walmart Greeter" outside in the backyard. Unlike the typical territorial behavior of male cats, Tyler welcomed stray cats into our yard.

With trepidation, I had my other cats tested for feline leukemia. I cried with happiness to learn that none of the others had become infected. I immediately had them immunized and they've all stayed clean to this day.

I feel honored to have had the privilege of loving Tyler and being loved by him for nine years. I will always cherish my party loving, gregarious, sweet and loyal, singing-challenged kitty. Tyler was truly one of a kind.

"HALEY"

Chapter 9
SCAREDY CAT

It was the start of the holiday season when I saw three tiny kittens dive into a dumpster at the retirement community where I work. I was sickened at the sight of those babies foraging for food, so I hid from them and waited until they left the dumpster. I maintained a safe distance and kept them in my line of sight until they returned to their feral mom and her companion. What a gorgeous array of feline specimens! There was a long-haired orange and white kitten, a brown tabby, and a tortoiseshell, like the mama cat. Tortoiseshells, called "torties" for short, have multi-colored orange, brown, black, beige, and gold fur with amber colored eyes.

I knew instantly I wanted to help these cats. I began feeding them every day and, as this was at the start of my feral cat journey, placed a call to the local feral cat advocacy group for assistance. I continued to feed the cats while I waited to hear back from the advocacy group. On Christmas morning I went to the property to feed my new charges and, just a few hundred feet inside the campus, one of the kittens lay dead on the pavement. I was horrified.

He had been run over by a car. He was the most beautiful of the kittens, too, with a luxuriously long orange and white coat, and green eyes. I was devastated.

I'd become quite attached to him and his siblings. The tears flowed as I picked him up and said to him, "My precious boy . . . what were you doing out here, so far from your mom and so close to the highway? I loved you so much; I'm so very sorry." My heart was broken. He's the kitten I would later posthumously name Austin Jr.

The advocacy group contacted me after the first of the year. I took their T-N-R course, and a volunteer showed me how to use their recommended humane traps. My priority was to trap the remaining two kittens, have them spayed/neutered, then foster and socialize them to pave the way for adoption. Chris with the San Antonio Feral Cat Coalition accompanied me on my first trapping excursion, and we caught the two kittens in short order.

The visit to the spay/neuter clinic revealed the two felines were both female. Carrie, the tortoiseshell, was more outgoing than her sister, Haley. I was able to socialize Carrie and place her with a no-kill shelter quickly. Haley, on the other hand, was a tough case. In thirty years of cat guardianship, Haley is by far the most bashful cat I have ever encountered. She took timidity to a whole new level. She was afraid of me, my other cats, the furniture, and as the saying goes, her own shadow.

Each baby step on her road to socialization felt like one step forward, one step back. Haley hid under the bed in my guest room for the first two weeks, venturing out only to eat and use the litterbox. I have since learned that it's recommended to crate a shy cat until she/he can be easily touched and picked up. Caging the cat allows easy access for socialization and prevents the animal from seeking hiding places in a room with open access.

I will never forget my attempts at teaching Haley to be comfortable with sitting on my lap and letting me stroke her. I would reassure her in a very soft voice, saying, "It feels good to be stroked; kitties like to be stroked." I was determined to somehow will her to socialization.

Eventually she became accustomed to our lap-sitting ritual. This routine then became her only comfort zone for interacting with me. If I tried to lift her off my lap, she would quickly scramble back on. I couldn't touch her or play with her anywhere else but on my lap.

I would laughingly ask her if she intended to spend the rest of her life sitting on my lap. Her answer was, apparently, a resounding "Yes!"

It was quite funny, cute, and yet totally exasperating!

By the time Haley was fully socialized and no longer panicky over any noise louder than two decibels, she was nearing twelve weeks old. I called several shelters every day in an attempt to find her a home, but none of the shelters would take her. They all told me there was no demand for kittens this age. The most desirable kittens are the younger ones, from six to eight weeks old. This was my first experience dealing with a shelter, and I was surprised to learn that a kitten is seen as being washed up at the tender age of 12 weeks.

Now that shelter placement was out of the question, I had to consider other options. I felt her age would also hinder adoption with the various cat adoption/rescue groups.

I decided that I had no choice but to adopt the green-eyed kitten myself. I had become quite fond of her as I patiently acquiesced to her shyness. I couldn't help but feel compassion for such a fearful animal. There was also a sweetness about her that was undeniably appealing. She communicated mainly with me through her eyes. Upon hearing my voice, Haley would squeeze her eyes almost shut and hold her gaze on me for long periods of time. I had a heart-to-heart talk with Haley and made my announcement: "Ok Haley, I guess you are going to join the family." And that was that.

I allowed her to assimilate into the household of five other cats at her own pace. She remained in the guest room, and I kept the door open for her to come and go as she pleased. My other cats must have sensed her timidity, too, as they didn't push her to interact with them.

Haley would venture outside her quarters, then quickly turn around and run back in upon seeing one of the other cats. Sometimes a loud noise would send her running for cover. As she explored each room, she cowered behind or under pieces of furniture when feeling frightened.

She spent most of her time hiding behind furniture. She might spend half a day hiding behind the sofa before feeling safe enough to venture on. It took Haley two weeks to travel to the other side of the house! She set a new record for "slow" cat exploration of my home—I've had new cats cover the same ground in less than two hours!

I was telling my friend, Mo, the story of how

Haley's prolonged socialization led to my decision to adopt her. Mo simply laughed and said, "Wow, Janet, she totally scammed you with the shyness routine. She saw her sister leave your home, and she didn't want to be next. She wanted to stay there with you."

I thought about Mo's assessment and feel she was partially right. I think Haley decided early on that she wanted to stay with me, and that she feared being returned to the feral cat colony. Haley didn't like being a feral cat, it just didn't work for her. She abhorred having to scrounge around for food. This is a kitty who likes knowing where her next meal is coming from.

One fact about Haley has become very clear to me over time. This feline is one of the most content cats I have ever owned. She shows me every day, as do all my rescues, how happy she is to have been rescued and cared for by me. It's all the thanks I need.

People talk about dogs smiling but rarely talk about cats forming expressions on their faces. Haley has taught me that cats do communicate their feelings via facial expressions. Haley gets a very concerned look on her face when she sees me sad or tearful. She goes into full red alert if she hears me sniffle. She moves closer to me, opens her eyes very wide, and fixes me in her stare. She completely tunes out everything around her. She will then continue her dedicated gaze until I verbally assure her that I'm ok. And she has to believe that I'm sincere, or she'll stay at her post, wide-eyed.

She's so attuned to me that when she hears me sniffle from a cold or allergy, she goes into concern mode and quickly comes to my side.

One of Haley's daily routines is to join me for breakfast, sitting on the table while I eat. I know this is very unsanitary but cat lovers will forgive me. (I promise, when I do have company over for dinner, I thoroughly sanitize the table.) She sleeps with me when the nights turn cooler, and some nights all three of my females crowd the bed.

I reached for Haley one night recently and found my two other females in bed with me also. I kissed all three and said, "Oh, we're having a girl's sleepover."

Haley has garnered one other award for unusual feline behavior, in my household at least. She is, hands down, the most skittish about going to the doctor of all the cats I have ever lived with. Not too long ago, she developed a health issue that required a trip to the veterinarian. She developed a case of Herculean strength when I picked her up to place her in the carrier! It was the most difficult cat transfer I've ever encountered, and that's saying a lot for all the ferals I've transported.

I remember telling myself at the time that one of us would surely get hurt. Wrestling with a stressed animal that has two more legs than I do, sharp teeth and nails, is never going to have a good outcome, especially for the human involved. It was quickly obvious I would be the one to suffer the physical ramifications. I should have had the foresight to wear my elbow length gardening gloves. I managed to deposit her into the carrier after MY Herculean strength kicked in. Cat wrangling, it turns out, is not my forte.

That clinic visit required a comprehensive examination and a battery of tests for poor Haley. I was then instructed to bring her back for a two-week follow-up visit.

That follow-up visit was doomed from the start. After three days of unsuccessful attempts to place her in the carrier, I called the doctor's office to seek advice. Could they give me a tuna flavored sedative to add to her food to make it easier to place her in the carrier? Of course they could, I was told.

Dr. Mixon advised me to confine Haley to her own room during this process. As it turns out, because she now associated me with the carrier, and the carrier with the doctor, it was impossible to pick her up to take her to a separate room. In fact, she had developed an intense fear of me, which I dearly hoped was temporary. If I moved within 15 feet of her, she would take off running. She ate her food with a rhythmic motion of eating two bites, then raising her head to look around to see if I was about to descend upon her, then lowered her head to eat some more and so on. If I made any small movement toward any of the food bowls, she fled.

I brought the sedative home and placed a small amount in her canned tuna. Haley walked over to the bowl, sniffed it, and promptly ran away. Over the next few days, I added the medicine to her food with the same failed result. After she rejected the tuna cocktail, I then offered her a fresh helping of food without the additive. She ate the unaltered food every time!

About two weeks passed before Haley allowed me to get within touching range again. It was clear she retained a very long memory of that fateful trip to the clinic and my sinister role in placing her in that carrier. Her comfort level with me wavered from one day to the next, and from one moment to the next. We could be in the midst of a kitty-pleasing petting session, and her demeanor would change in an instant from calm to fear. Haley would suddenly look at me with intense panic, run away, and hide for the rest of the day.

It took a full four weeks before Haley resumed a normal relationship with me. Thankfully, the symptoms that required the doctor's visit didn't return. My sister and I joked that Haley healed herself so she never had to go back.

There will come a time in the not too distant future, though, that I will have to take Haley and the other kitties in for a teeth cleaning. I am planning to put a very solid "cat transfer to carrier" policy in place, which may require me to implement a two-woman cat-wrangling procedure. While I have laughed about this with friends and in the writing of this disaster, the whole ordeal was as stressful for me as it was for her.

Haley has been very welcoming to our newest addition, Carrie Ann. Carrie Ann is a rambunctious nine-month-old kitten who gobbles down her food and runs over to eat out of Haley's bowl. Haley graciously steps back and allows Carrie Ann to take whatever she wants. To help out my submissive Haley, I have learned to simply give Carrie Ann more food.

To this day, Haley remains the most bashful of the brood. The first time my friend Debbie cared for the kitties while I was out of town, she reported to me that Haley was too timid to come into the kitchen to eat. Naturally, she was hungry, but her fear of Debbie outweighed her desire to eat.

Haley's meal includes a special treat, and Debbie didn't want to leave it in her bowl for fear one of the other cats would consume Haley's portion. Debbie was certainly listening to my cat babysitting instructions when I described my biggest male, Tyler, as the clean up guy. Tyler quickly eats his food and rushes over to dine at the other cat's bowls.

Debbie reported to me that she actually took Haley's prized helping to her in my bedroom and placed the bowl just under the edge of the bed. My bed, mostly under it, had become Haley's refuge when she felt threatened by strangers. Each day, Debbie patiently waited for Haley to eat the tuna and then carried the bowl back to the kitchen for her share of the dry food.

The next time Debbie babysat, Haley ventured

closer to the kitchen and watched from the safety of the dining room while Debbie fed the other cats. If Debbie made eye contact with her, she would retreat to the bedroom just as fast as her legs could carry her. By the third time my friend took care of the cats, Haley decided she could trust Debbie, and ate with the other kitties in the kitchen. Haley continues to be initially shy toward Debbie upon her entry into our home, but after a few moments of evaluating the situation, Haley realizes that Debbie is the same human who is her friend and allows her back "in".

When I returned from a recent trip, Haley did her usual welcome home routine. It started with a reconnaissance mission through the living room. She moved toward me with a slow and deliberate gate, stalking me with a frontwards then sideways walk, occasionally veering off path to hide behind a piece of furniture. Nearing the completion of her mission, she seemed to be asking me with her fear-enlarged eyes, *"Is it safe? Is it you, Mom, is it really you?"*

Haley has been with me now for five years. The bountiful loyalty, companionship and affection she demonstrates for me every day more than makes up for the occasional stress she creates with her extreme timidity.

"JOEY"

Chapter 10
HE'S ALL BOY

Joey is decidedly the character of my brood. If he were a child, Joey would be affectionately described as "all boy". Friends depict him as full of himself, the daredevil, life of the party. He is all of that and more. He is a very busy cat, as you can see from the footprint of his typical day.

Joey's daily to-do list would look something like

this:

1.   *Eat breakfast.*

2.   *Ignore Mom's admonitions against scratching the white chair. Ignore the four scratching posts Mom has scattered conveniently around the house and sharpen my claws on the white chair and the matching footrest. I'm resting my feet on it, aren't I?*

3.   *Use the litterbox as often as possible just to kick out five times as much litter as the other cats.*

4.   *Wrestle with Carrie Ann, then groom Carrie Ann.*

5.   *Wrestle with Haley, then groom Haley.*

6.   *Jump to the top of the refrigerator and onto the top of the cabinets. Precariously walk among Mom's antique bottles and baskets and try not to break anything. At least as far as she knows.*

7.   *Eat a mid morning snack—hey, a guy burns a lot of calories keeping this busy.*

8.   *Jump on top of the kitchen table from a dead run, slide across the table, land on the placemat, and fall off the table.*

9.   *Check out what Mom's doing in the office and lie down on the middle of the computer keyboard.*

10.   *Move to the side of her inbox after being chased off the computer.*

11.   *Jump on her lap after knocking the inbox*

to the floor.

12.   Sneak up on Kelly and scare her while she is using the litterbox.

13.   Follow Kelly into the pantry and hold her hostage until Mom notices that both of us are missing.

14.   Time for din-din—must keep fueled for my nighttime shenanigans.

15.   Run through the house shrieking, which is cat speak for, "Who wants to play?"

16.   Keep Mommy company while she does her weight training.

17.   Shower Mom with kisses, neck nuzzle,s and lots of purring. Better to beg forgiveness later than to seek permission.

18.   Feeling a little sleepy. Mom's bed is going to feel really good after such an industrious day!

Joey was my fourth rescue, and as with the rest of the kitties, he was an unplanned addition to the family. I recently told a friend that if I ever have the hankering for a new cat, all I have to do is walk outside my front door. This is a sad but true commentary on the way many folks treat animals in my city—as disposable objects.

I was driving down my street, and a handsome grey cat with a mangled-looking tail crossed in front of my car. My heart rose to my throat at the gruesome sight. I quickly pulled over to better survey the situation, then got out of the car and knelt down on the sidewalk close to the cat.

I called out to him, saying, "Come here darling, I'll take care of you."

He walked right up to me and nuzzled my hand as I reached down to pet him.

His tail was completely stripped of fur, and was bloody and fleshy looking. I had a hard time even looking at it. I wondered what could have happened to this friendly, handsome cat. I was struck by how normal he was acting, not appearing to be in distress. I quickly lifted him up and put him in the car for the short ride to my home for transfer to a cat carrier.

In the short distance to my home, the kitty became frightened and jumped from the front to the back, the back to the front, and so on. This resulted in some badly blood-stained upholstery—on my one-day old interior car cleaning. Note to self: keep a cat carrier in the trunk and be done with it.

I called the doctors office from the car and told them I was bringing in a kitty that needed immediate attention. Thankfully, the staff knows me and my penchant for helping strays pretty well by now. I was told to come right over.

Dr. Mixon explained that the only way to treat the kitty was to amputate his tail. He would have a short bobtail, like a Manx. If he didn't amputate, infection would soon set in, travel throughout his body and kill him. Dr. Mixon theorized that the injury was either caused by a car running over his tail, or he may have fallen asleep near a car engine that singed all the hair off.

Dr. Mixon also mentioned what a handsome feline he was. Yes, I had to agree. The cat was an 18-month-old short-haired grey tabby, with pale, white markings and light green eyes. I consented to the surgery, and this approval essentially sealed the deal for me to keep him. I rationalized my new "acquisition" because I'd successfully held my cat population to three cats for four consecutive months.

The next day I named him Joey. I thought it a suitable name for a former street warrior. Joey has an infectious personality that makes a lasting impression on everyone who's lucky enough to meet him.

As personable with humans as he was, Joey was a very difficult cat to assimilate into the household. For starters, he was collared while his tail healed to prevent him from chewing off the bandages. He was an intact male when I found him, and I wanted to delay neutering for awhile to give him a chance to recover from the amputation.

This decision proved to be a mistake. The large amount of testosterone in his body caused Joey to be very aggressive with my two females. Of course, he was just being a normal intact male, but he relentlessly chased after them, even while wearing the large collar. It was both a funny and shocking sight. In telling my friend Judy about this, she commented that he must have looked rather scary to the other kitties, running at them with that weird collar.

That's an understatement! I spent a lot of time refereeing fights and pulling Joey off the girls. Kelly was scared to death of him and took to living under my bed, only coming out to eat and use the litterbox.

In one instance, Joey was standing on my bed with Haley cornered under the bed. She looked at me with sheer terror in her eyes as if to say, *"Mommy, do something."*

I was so frustrated with Joey that I got close to him and screamed at him to back off. I hated myself for doing it, but I was totally exasperated; at that moment, I wasn't in control of my emotions.

What happened next shocked me. Joey momentarily forgot about his prisoner and turned around to look at me. He glared at me as he deliberately moved closer and bit my arm. It was clearly an act of retaliation. He quickly returned to his post to continue his torment of Haley. I was more intrigued than upset by his actions. I intuitively made a number of observations about his behavior. I found him impressive in many ways.

I interpreted his actions as a sign of intelligence and assertiveness. He was sending me the message that he would respond in kind to aggressive behavior. A short time later, all was forgiven and forgotten. Joey was back to his affectionate self with me. A vigorous head butt said it all. I had never, in thirty years of pet guardianship, experienced retaliation from an animal.

I had to respect that. I also knew the high testosterone level in his body was a contributing factor. The experience made me realize that the other kitties and I needed a vacation from Joey.

I called the doctor's office and made arrangements for him to be neutered. Dr. Mike advised me that, yes, the surgery would significantly decrease the aggressive behavior toward my two females. I could expect to see immediate improvement, with all the aggression dissipating within fourteen days—the amount of time needed for the testosterone to vacate his body. It was time anyway to take him in for removal of the tail stitches. I made arrangements for the office to board him for a few days post surgery as part of our "break".

The next day, I visited Joey a few hours after his surgery, but he was too groggy to recognize me. On day two, I visited again, and Dr. Mixon accompanied me into the cat room. Dr. Mike pointed to the crate that held Joey. I could barely see him as he was hunkered down at the back of the cage. I called out his name rather slowly and loudly while approaching him, "J O E Y!"

He sprang to his feet and rushed to the front of the cage, answering me with a loud "Muh Muh Meow".

Dr. Mixon exclaimed, "He speaks! This is the first time he's uttered a sound."

Joey had reached another cat milestone. I had never heard a cat utter word sounds other than the various nuances they make with their meows. I couldn't open that cage door fast enough. Joey and I shared a mutual lovefest for the next few minutes. He showered me with loud purring, rigorous nuzzling, and lots of kisses. If cats could smile, this feline would have been grinning ear to ear. He was in kitty heaven.

I think he thought he'd been abandoned and would never see me again. In telling my friends about our reunion and his opening "word meow," two of them commented it was as if he was saying mama, followed by the meow.

Joey had a very successful homecoming. As the doctor had predicted, the surgery melted away all of Joey's aggressiveness. The neutering made him calmer and happier. It allowed the "fun" Joey to become his dominant personality.

I call Joey my "love machine". His creativity in expressing his affection for me continues to amaze me. One of his "Joey specials" is to jump to the top of my recliner behind my head and nuzzle my neck. He has recently added a part two to this routine. After the warm up nuzzle, he then massages my shoulders by "making biscuits." This is the term used to describe the kneading cats do with their paws to mark us with their scent. Then there is the Joey kiss. He gently wraps his mouth around my nose or a part of my cheek.

While I was working out recently on my incline weight bench, he surprised me by leaping to the top of the bench and proceeded to perform the "Joey special." It takes some real balance to simultaneously straddle the bench at just the right angle, dole out the affection, and not fall off.

Joey and my newest addition, ten-month-old Carrie Ann, have recently taken to greeting me at the door. Joey takes the lead, and the small fry hangs back a little. They make for a very fine welcome home, this unconventional duo with his thirteen pounds and her six pound petite frame.

They've become fast friends as both are new additions to the family and they're close in age. Joey is busy showing Carrie Ann the ropes. Much to my chagrin, he taught her to scale the refrigerator and the armoire in the den. On Carrie Ann's second exploration of the armoire, she knocked over and broke one of my favorite pieces of pottery from an antique dealer in San Diego. He has tried to show her how to jump from the refrigerator to the cabinets, but so far, she seems fearful of attempting such a large leap.

Joey has invented a new game he plays with his Aunt Debbie. While she's seated at the kitchen table, he lies down near her feet and wraps his paws around one of her legs. The fun begins for Joey when she tries to get up, because he increases his grip on her, effectively holding her hostage. Joey is never ready to end the game, so we have to physically pry his paws from her leg when it's time for her to leave.

One of the special games I play with Joey is to try

to sneak up on him while he is napping to give him a surprise mommy kiss. Being a member of the feline persuasion, he always hears me approaching, and so effectively wins the game. He lifts his head and greets me with several infectious meows, as if to say, "Better luck next time, Mom".

One recent evening, Joey ran screeching through the house and into the guest room. He fell silent once he entered the room. This space also doubles as the cat foster room, and is outfitted with a six-foot table and some crates. After about a minute, he emerged from the room meowing happily.

Soon, he again ran squealing into the guest room and retreated into momentary silence. He completed the routine for the second time by sauntering out, meowing joyously. By the third rendition, my curiosity got the better of me. I wanted to know what in that room was eliciting such delight for Joey. I waited for him to enter and fall silent, and then I quickly followed him. There stood Joey in all his feline glory, proudly preening at the top of one of the crates. He'd positioned himself at the highest point in the room.

No wonder he was so happy with himself! Cats instinctively derive pleasure from looking down on their environment, allowing them to watch for predators and prey. Joey's special take on life and his joy in conquering make him a daily delight. I look forward to many more years filled with love, kitty massages, and silly antics from my Joey.

"CARRIE ANN"

Chapter 11
SAVING CARRIE ANN

H ow does a six-pound furball dictate the serving of breakfast for five cats and a human? Carrie Ann's formula for success is as follows: The moment I step into the kitchen she follows me around, whining EH, EH, EH, EH, EH, EH.

Yes, that's right. It's not a meow. It's an EH.

I think she's saying, *"Mom, hurry up and feed me. I want to eat RIGHT NOW. No, you may not make your* coffee before feeding me."

If I don't get the lead out fast enough to suit her, she cranks it up a notch: Ms. Bossy then swats at my legs, as if to say, *"Hello, excuse me, I'm right here. Feed me first. Those other cats can wait. Make it fast, Mom. I'm starving to death over here."*

My other cats have become quite tolerant of the whole spectacle. They wisely move out of Carrie Ann's way while she's flitting around at my heels. Needless to say, her technique works every morning—you can be sure the baby girl gets fed first. I don't mind so much that Carrie Ann bosses me around at breakfast, but I would prefer that she first allow me to make my coffee. And God knows we could all do with a little less EH-ING!

I tolerate her demanding behavior because I'm thankful to see Carrie Ann so happy, healthy, and confident. The assertive Carrie Ann is a delightful contrast to the timid young feline I first encountered. My friend Chris had accompanied me on a trapping venture to collect one of my more challenging cats. While he was at the front of the property setting up a trap, I went to the back of the property to set up a second trap. I had no sooner set the trap when I heard a faint, rather pathetic-sounding meow. I turned around to see a small cat walking toward me. She was not afraid of me, so I knew instantly she wasn't feral. When I got closer to her, I saw that her eyes were moist. She looked as if she'd been crying. I've experienced this phenomenon in a cat only one other time.

In addition to being moved by her desperate wailing, I was struck by her beauty. This feline was a long-haired brown tabby with yellow eyes. I'd seen a long-haired tabby only one other time, and that one had the more common green cat eyes. It was obvious the diminutive feline was starving. I guessed her age to be between five and seven months. She sniffed the food in the trap and walked right in. I showed my catch to Chris as she continued her desperate calls from inside the cage. I was moved by extreme pity.

There was despondency in her voice that I hadn't encountered before in a cat. Chris commented that she wasn't feral because she was "talking to us." Feral cats are usually silent. They don't meow to communicate with humans until they develop some level of socialization and comfort with their human caretakers.

Chris and I discussed potential options for both the short and long-term fate of the cat. For the short term, I would foster her until one of the cat advocacy groups could find her a forever home. It would have been cruel to return an adoptable stray to a feral cat colony.

Of course, the first order of business would be a trip to the spay/neuter clinic in the morning. At this point, I didn't know the sex of the cat, but I assumed that she was intact, as are most strays.

Upon removing the kitten from the trap to transfer her to a cage, I touched her underside and felt nipples. I then touched the sides of her stomach and looked at her tummy from both sides. Her belly was large and rock hard. I knew instantly she was pregnant. I felt so bad for this little girl. She looked like a kitten herself, and she was going to have babies. No wonder she was crying. She had a lot to cry about.

The little feline was alone, pregnant and starving. This would be my first time taking a pregnant female in to be spayed. I knew the standard of care for a pregnant female is to terminate the pregnancy. When I picked her up the next day after her surgery, my heart sank when I read the doctor's report: "pregnant female, five fetuses aborted." I managed to hold myself together until I got home. I knew of course that she would be having an abortion, but, somehow, calling it a pregnancy termination was easier to bear.

I got her settled into her temporary quarters in my garage, and that's when the dam broke! I cried for her unborn kittens, and for her, wondering how she had come to be alone at the feral cat colony. I imagined that her previous caretakers had abandoned her when they discovered she was knocked up. I cried also for the miserable life that all intact female stray and feral cats must endure. Intact females can deliver as many as three litters a year.

Their malnourished bodies barely have time to recover before they become pregnant again. It's a myth that a nursing mom can't become pregnant. The average litter size is three to five kittens, and the majority of kittens born in the wild don't survive their first year. They succumb to exposure from the elements, disease, or attacks from predator animals.

I moved the pint-sized girl into the guest room after a couple of days. She soon grew restless in the cage, so I released her and gave her free run of the room. She began to act strangely when I touched her food bowl. She hissed at me and lunged forward as if to scare me away. I was puzzled. She was trying to communicate something to me, but what?

Little did I know that this would become the most vexing foster cat challenge of my life. She became more and more agitated at mealtime when I reached down to pick up her empty bowl. The hissing and lunging behavior quickly escalated to grabbing and clawing at my arms. If I didn't back away, she would shriek loudly, jumping and clawing at my legs. After enduring several days of bloodied arms, I began to wear my elbow length gardening gloves to feed her. The same behavior carried over to the touching of her water bowl. I was keenly aware that this aggressive behavior dissipated after feeding time. She demonstrated her affection for me by frequent nuzzling and purring. She enjoyed long play sessions with me and seemed grateful for the toys loaned to her by my three cats.

What was it about the feeding ritual that triggered

this agitation? I drew on the psychotherapy experience I had garnered early in my career as a crisis and short-term therapy counselor. I realized she was exhibiting panic and anxiety behaviors as a result of cumulative starvation. Each time I picked up her bowls, she was afraid she would never see them again. It was as if she was trying to tell me: *"Please don't take away my food and water. I don't want to be hungry and thirsty again."*

I began to bring the food and water supplies into her room so I wouldn't have to remove the bowls from her sight. This change produced an immediate decrease in the agitation. She watched my actions like a hawk and quickly learned which container held the food supply. The panic resumed each time she observed me removing the food container from the room.

Ok, baby girl, I thought to myself. *I will use an even larger food container, and it will remain in your room where you can keep an eye on it.* Her food anxieties dissipated after a week. This was a huge relief as it was quite stressful to watch her endure such agony. Helping her to recover from the trauma required a lot of time and patience on my part. My feelings of triumph would be short-lived.

A few days later, she began to exhibit panic behaviors over a new issue. At the conclusion of feeding and play sessions, the action of me leaving her room triggered significant anxiety. The agitation started as soon as I stood up. The moment I began walking to the door, the feline's behavior escalated into a full meltdown. This time there was no clawing of the arms.

She shrieked loudly as she desperately clawed and jumped at my legs. I instinctively knew that she was trying to prevent me from leaving. I realized it was a traumatic reaction to a "fear of abandonment." I believe this beautiful little stray had been alone and frightened for some time before she landed at the feral cat colony. She was communicating to me the only way she could: *"Please don't leave me. I don't want to be alone. I am afraid you will not come back if you leave this room. Please, please don't leave me."*

I couldn't believe I had another behavioral issue to contend with. I gave myself a quick pep talk. Since I'd successfully treated her food anxieties, I was determined to alleviate this issue as well. The strategy included longer and more frequent visitations. I distracted her with food when it was time for me to leave the room. The new routine delayed my departure for work each morning by thirty minutes.

The new formula decreased her panic attacks. It then dawned on me that her guest room residence kept her isolated from my companionship day and night. This arrangement was feeding her fear of abandonment. I decided to alternate spending nights with her in the guest room with nights in my bedroom. At least two of my four cats sleep in my bedroom every night. I had to juggle meeting the kitten's needs without too much disruption to the routine of the resident cats. Cat caretakers everywhere know that cats crave routine. Spending nights with her in the guest room made her very happy and seemed to further quell the panic attacks.

The first night in her room, I instinctively lifted her onto the bed with me thinking she might enjoy a play and cuddle session before lights out. Much to my surprise, she wasn't comfortable being on the bed. She seemed frightened and immediately jumped down. I then realized that—unlike my spoiled cats— she wasn't accustomed to being on a bed.

I'm guessing her previous family hadn't allowed her to have bed privileges. After about ten days of alternating my nights with her in the guest room, the abandonment-fueled panic attacks ceased completely.

With the psychological trauma behind us, I started to think about taking her in to see Dr. Mixon for the necessary shots to help ready her for adoption. I then had a lightbulb moment. Placing her for adoption would trigger a relapse of her abandonment anxiety. A new environment would also risk a resumption of the food and water panic attacks.

I could explain to a new guardian how to handle her food deprivation and abandonment trauma, but would a prospective caretaker want to take this on? Would someone be willing to adopt a "crazy" cat? Would another person possess the patience, compassion and training to see her through this entire trauma? I decided that no one else could be expected to handle these challenges.

Placing her in a shelter would have resulted in a revolving door of failed, short-term adoptions, each one exacerbating the state of her fragile psyche. How could I do that to her? Of course, I couldn't. My only solution was to adopt the small fry. And besides, with all we had been through together, I'd become very attached to the kitty.

The successful treatment and resolution of her psychological issues made me reflect about all the pets dumped at animal shelters. An inability to deal with pet behavioral issues is the number one reason that owners surrender their pets to shelters. Many of these surrenders would be unnecessary if people would read up on kitten and puppy care and training, familiarize themselves with the behavioral traits of dogs and different dog breeds, and consult their veterinarians for advice in resolving the issues.

Shelters are filled with dogs whose owners didn't understand their "pack mentality" and their need for human companionship. Spending more time with the dog or providing a companion dog alleviates the common complaints of destructive behavior by a lonely or bored canine. There has been discussion about our own City Animal Care Services providing pet care information and advice to people calling the City to come and pick up their problem pets. Around the nation, many animal shelters regularly dispense telephone advice and hold educational pet care clinics. This is just one cost-effective strategy to prevent shelter over-crowding.

Now that I would be adopting "small fry", the next order of business was to give her a name. I decided that she needed both a pretty and stylish name to match her exceptional good looks. One of her distinguishing features is the lioness mane that frames her neck. She has a star-shaped marking on her forehead that exactly matches her amber colored eyes.

I decided I would call her Carrie, for the Carrie Bradshaw character on "Sex and the City." Then I gave her the middle name of Ann to honor Carrie Ann Inaba, one of the judges from "Dancing with the Stars." And so, Carrie Ann the kitty was officially named!

Now that Carrie Ann was joining the family, we went to see Dr. Mixon for the required shots and tests. She would need to be declared disease-free and receive the usual preventive immunizations before I could introduce her to my other cats. I told Dr. Mixon and the staff about the ordeal of treating her fears of abandonment, and the anxiety attacks over food and water deprivation. I asked the doctor if he'd ever heard of a cat having this similar condition. Dr. Mixon is a cat expert, having previously worked in an all-feline clinic. He was amazed by the story and declared that he'd never heard of even one other similar case.

Dr. Mixon pronounced Carrie Ann to be a healthy

nine-month-old. That meant she was only seven and a half months old when she became pregnant. The poor little girl had experienced hard times for someone so young. On the bright side, she was declared disease-free, so it was time to introduce her to my other cats.

I started by bringing Joey in for short, supervised visitations, and the gregarious Joey was only too happy to comply. Of all the cats, Joey had shown the most interest in the mysterious cat in the bedroom. He already knew her scent when I introduced them face-to-face because he'd been playing "pawsies" with her under the bedroom door. In fact, one of the proven methods for introducing a new cat into a household is to keep the new cat in a separate room until the resident cats have all had an opportunity to pick up the new kitty's scent by poking their paws under the closed door and playing "tag, you're it."

My other three cats that have seniority over Joey didn't appear to be playing pawsies with Carrie Ann, though. I imagined their nonchalant behavior inferred they'd already accepted the new upstart: *"Well, it looks like Mom's bringing another new cat into the household. No big deal."*

Carrie Ann blended into our home pretty easily and became fast friends with Joey.

Carrie Ann is also very devoted to me. Like my other rescued cats, she displays her gratitude every day, through a number of "mommy-appreciation rituals". One of the most endearing involves her walking around the house—meowing—to find me after she awakens from a nap. The post-nap meow is different from her normal meow; it's very distinctive. It sounds something like the "wah" cry that cartoon babies make.

The little girl wants me to pet her and love on her when she's feeling vulnerable. I find this routine very touching. It reminds me of a toddler waking up from a nap and immediately wanting to be comforted by her mother.

Sometimes before falling to sleep she'll signal me with some meows to come and cuddle her while she's settling down. And then there are the Carrie kisses, where she licks my hand until I can no longer tolerate that sand paper feel on my skin and have to pull away.

Unfortunately, the small fry has a dark side. I say this tongue-and-cheek, but she is possessive of me with my two other females. Carrie Ann allows me precious little "alone time" with the other kitties. As soon as she sees me with one of her competitors, she moves into close proximity to monitor the interaction or to join the petting/playing activities.

As a matter of fact, all three of my females are possessive, and all are rescues. I've had females in the past who were not possessive and weren't rescues. There must be something about the rescue distinction that triggers this behavior. Perhaps the gratitude toward the rescuer creates a kind of attachment that manifests in possessiveness and a fear of losing the relationship.

Carrie Ann moves very fast. One of her favorite activities is to help Mommy make the bed. She dives in and out of the covers and bites at the covers while I'm trying to get my day started. I have almost given up trying to "beat her" into the bedroom to get a running head start before she joins me. If I see her in the litterbox, I hurry over to the bed before she realizes what I'm doing. Four times out of five, by the time I reach the bed she's already there, resting comfortably, waiting for the games to begin. I don't know how she does it—it's an amazing and inexplicable feat. Remember the old Bugs Bunny and Elmer Fudd cartoons? The two would depart the same location at the same time and have a contest as to who would arrive first at their destination.

Bugs Bunny would win every time. Poor Ol' Elmer would arrive tired and panting. Bugs would be chewing on that infamous carrot as he exclaimed, "Eh, What's Up Doc?"

I have a sneaking suspicious that I'm poor old Elmer Fudd.

I didn't expect to find Carrie Ann at the feral cat colony that day. I feed at that location every weekend and my co-worker Janice feeds on weekdays. Neither of us had ever seen Carrie Ann before that Saturday. I will never know how she ended up there or how long she'd been there.

My instincts tell me she arrived just in time for me

to find her; I believe it was no accident that we met. I trust that God put her in my path that day, knowing she was in desperate need of help and exactly what kind of person was needed to help her.

The rescuer needed to be patient, compassionate, and an experienced counselor! The joy that Carrie Ann brings to my life every day far outweighs the emotional stress I endured while saving her.

"RORY"

Lagniappe

C at guardians, cat lovers, and feral cat colony managers will enjoy reviewing this list of resources. Included are local organizations that will benefit readers living in the San Antonio area and other resources that will be of value to a broader audience.

- AlleyCatAllies.org. The national authority on stray and feral cats.

- San Antonio Feral Cat Coalition, sanantonioferalcats.org. This nonprofit organization is dedicated to reducing the overpopulation of outside cats in the San Antonio area through rescue and Trap-Neuter-Return (TNR). Community outreach educates the public about stray and feral cats and the need to spay/neuter pets. Support services assist colony caretakers as resources allow. Advocacy works to protect cats from cruelty and help colony feeders with legally-based solutions.

- SonyaFitzpatrick.com. Radio Show Host, SiriusXM, Animal Intuition, TV Host of Animal Planet's *The Pet Psychic* and *Pet Psychic Encounters*, Author of *What the Animals Tell Me* and *Cat Talk*

- Craig Brestrup, PHD. Author, Disposable Animals: Ending the Tragedy of Throwaway Pets

- Cathy Rosenthal. Send pet stories and questions to cathy@petpundit.com. You can read her blog, *Animals Matter*, at http://blog.mysanantonio.com/animals. Ms. Rosenthal's weekly column, *Animals Matter*, runs on Tuesdays in the San Antonio Express-News. Cathy is the author of several children's books.

- TexasVeterinaryHospitals.com. Dr. Mike Mixon, cat expert and the lead veterinarian for all my owned and feral cats.

Acknowledgments

I wish to thank Book Club members Susan Jarvis, Diane Layne, and Richard Layne for their enthusiastic and unwavering support of me during the writing of this book. I am very grateful for cat advocate extraordinaire, Chris Montgomery. He was my "trapping mentor" early on and continues to advise and inspire me.

About the Author

Janet S. Dumas lives in San Antonio, Texas and is a semi-retired medical social worker. She enjoys writing, fitness, gardening, and spending time with friends and family. She has been a cat afficionado for over 40 years, and her love for animals led to an unintended journey into cat advocacy fourteen years ago. Janet is passionate about improving the lives of stray and feral cats. She enjoys caring for these vulnerable felines while educating pet owners and well, anyone who will listen, about the need for spay/neuter and our responsibility to care for God's creatures.

We hope you enjoyed Janet S. Dumas
Blessings from My Cats

COULD YOU TAKE A MOMENT TO GIVE THE BOOK
A SHORT REVIEW ON AMAZON.COM? YOUR REVIEWS
MEAN THE WORLD TO OUR AUTHORS, AND HELP THEM
EXPAND THEIR AUDIENCE AND THEIR VOICE.
THANK YOU SO MUCH!

Find links to Blessings from My Cats *and all our great books
on Amazon or at www.whochainsyou.com.*

Children's Books for Cat Lovers
FROM WHO CHAINS YOU BOOKS

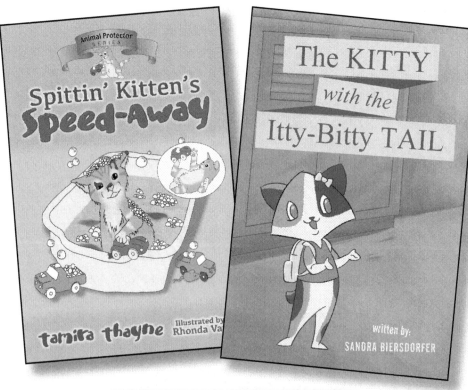

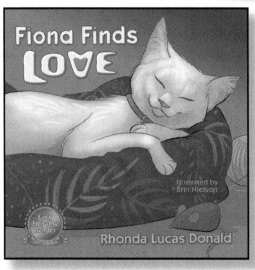

Also from WCY for Cat Lovers

IN RESCUING CATS I LOST MY MIND BUT FOUND MY SOUL, *by Cheryl Kwasigroch*

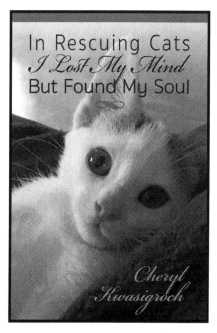

Cheryl Kwasigroch writes based on personal experience, and with a deep understanding of the feline mind—as well as the knowledge that a cat is a very special animal whose health and medical needs are quite different from those of other pets.

What does it involve to do rescue work with cats, or just be a caring cat adopter? In these 19 short yet heartwarming stories, different cats as well as the people in their lives struggle to understand one another.

Travel the feline world with these remarkable stories of inspirational cats. You may shed a tear along the way, but in the end we hope you will find yourself wanting to do more for our beautiful and often misunderstood companions.

Read more and order from whochainsyou.com, Amazon, and other outlets.

Also from Who Chains You Books

MORE RESCUE SMILES: BEST-LOVED ANIMAL TALES OF RESILIENCE & REDEMPTION

The heart of the animal rescue world lies in its stories—of freedom, of love, and of sacrifice by those who not only acknowledge but embrace the human-animal bond and its wondrous gifts.

In our second rescue story compilation, Who Chains You Books is pleased to share a glimpse into the emotional lives of animal rescuers and the living beings they hold close. Join us for another helping of heartwarming anecdotes, as Clancy triumphs, Tallulah escapes, Alex survives, and a host of other animals steal our hearts.

Through these stories, you'll get a behind-the-scenes look into the relationships between rescuers and not only dogs and cats, but horses, cows, pigs, birds, and even a ferret, in this delightful second installment of *Rescue Smiles*.

We hope you're as captivated by the kinship between human and animal as we are . . .*Read more and order from whochainsyou.com, Amazon, and other outlets.*

About Who Chains You Books

LOVE ANIMALS? WELCOME! OUR BOOKS APPLAUD ANIMALS AND THOSE WHO CARE FOR THEM, AND CELEBRATE THE CONNECTION BETWEEN HUMANS AND OUR NON-HUMAN FRIENDS.

At Who Chains You, we publish books for those who believe people—and animals—deserve to be free.

We seek to educate, entertain, and share gripping plights of the animals we serve and those who rescue and stand in their stead. At our deepest levels, we explore what chains we humans must break within ourselves in order to free the animals.

Read more about us at whochainsyou.com.

Made in the USA
Columbia, SC
28 November 2020